105

The Salish People and the Lewis and Clark Expedition

The Salish People

and the

Lewis and Clark Expedition

Salish-Pend d'Oreille Culture Committee
and Elders Cultural Advisory Council
Confederated Salish and Kootenai Tribes

UNIVERSITY OF NEBRASKA PRESS   LINCOLN AND LONDON

*Publication of this book was made possible
with support from the* Confederated Salish and Kootenai Tribes, *the*
Montana Lewis and Clark Bicentennial Commission, *the*
American Public Land Exchange Company, *the*
Plum Creek Foundation, *and the*
Dennis and Phyllis Washington Foundation.
This project is funded in part by a grant from the
Montana Committee for the Humanities,
an affiliate of the National Endowment for the Humanities.

Montana Committee for the Humanities

Acknowledgments for previously published
material appear on pages 191–95

Library of Congress
Cataloging-in-Publication Data

The Salish people and the Lewis and Clark Expedition/Salish-Pend
d'Oreille Culture Committee and Elders Cultural Advisory Council,
Confederated Salish and Kootenai Tribes.
    p.   cm.
Includes bibliographical references and index.
ISBN 0-8032-4311-1 (cloth: alk. paper)
1. Salish people—History. 2. Salish people—Social life and customs.
3. Lewis and Clark Expedition (1804–1806) I. Confederated Salish
and Kootenai Tribes. Salish-Pend d'Oreille Culture Committee. II.
Confederated Salish and Kootenai Tribes. Elders Cultural Advisory
Council.
E99.S2S26 2005
978.6004'979435—dc22
2004028602

Designed and set in Sqeksa Pablo (created by Salish Kootenai College,
Pablo MT) and Adobe Garamond by R. W. Boeche. Printed by Friesens.

Frontispiece: *The Day Lewis and Clark Came.*
    Oil painting by Tony Sandoval, 2003.

Esqey̓ ye q̓ey̓min
x̣ʷl̓ qe es pute^ʔm qe x̣ʷlčmussn
u yetłx̣ʷa sqlqélix̣ʷ
u y̓e puti^ʔ čn̓en̓n̓es.

This book is written
because we respect our ancestors
and the people here today
and the generations yet to come.

Contents

10,000 Years Indigenous People—200 Years Lewis and Clark, number 6, by Corky Clairmont, 2001.

INTRODUCTION
Tribal Voices
and Tribal History

On September 4, 1805, a large band of Salish people was encamped at one of the traditional places in the upper Bitterroot Valley—a place called Kʷtił Ṗupⱡm̓, meaning Coming Out into a Big Open Place. Non-Indians know this place as Ross's Hole, the large upland prairie on the East Fork of the Bitterroot River, in what is now western Montana. On that day two hundred years ago, our people were gathered there as countless generations of ancestors had been before them. Dozens of lodges were set up in the high open valley, and some four hundred people and more than that number of horses were enjoying the warm, sunny days and cold nights at the western base of the Pintlar Range. Since it was September, they would be harvesting łxʷłó (chokecherries), which grew in great profusion in the area. The women would pound the cherries with stone hammers, form the mush into patties, and then dry the patties and store them for use as food throughout the long winter. The people would also be gathering stečcxʷ (red osier dogwood berries) and pasturing their fine horses on the abundant grasses of Kʷtił Ṗupⱡm̓, before moving on toward the plains for the fall buffalo hunt.

Pend d'Oreille elder John Peter Paul at Kʷtíł Ṗupⱡm̓, September 1998.

On that September day our scouts spotted a group of pale-skinned men approaching the encampment. Our people later learned that these strangers were the members of the Lewis and Clark expedition.

In most non-Indian accounts, the expedition's arrival marks the beginning of the history of Montana. But as we will see in the pages that follow, Lewis and Clark were much less discoverers than visitors, venturing into the territory of a sovereign native nation—a tribal world that was older, richer, and more complex than the expedition members could have possibly imagined.

This book was written as the bicentennial of the Lewis and Clark expedition approached. In part, it is a tribal response to the growing frenzy of media attention and scholarly interest in the history of the expedition. For all the rising flood of books and articles, films and television programs, events and historical exhibits on Lewis and Clark, few accounts have given much attention to the people who happened to live in the vast areas suddenly claimed by the United States following the Louisiana Purchase of 1803. Few have offered much of real substance on the central issue in this history: the relationship between the expedition and the native people of western North America.

Because of the diversity of indigenous peoples, native perspectives on the Lewis and Clark expedition are best revealed through the particular lens of each tribe. This book explores the historical meaning of Lewis and Clark within the context of Salish culture and history—the Salish relationship with their homeland, the details of the Salish encounter with the expedition, and the placement of this encounter within the larger flow of Salish history before and after 1805. Rather than examining the role of native people within the history of the expedition, we are examining the role of the expedition within the history of our tribe—within the history of one tribe's struggle for cultural and political survival over the past several centuries.

For the past century Lewis and Clark have figured prominently at the beginning of nearly every U.S. history textbook. Even today, the word *discovery* pervades most Lewis and Clark materials, and it animates the package tours shuttling visitors to every point along the expedition's route. The expedition is still cast as the genesis of the United States as a transcontinental nation. This explains some of the powerful emotions surrounding the bicentennial and the desire of many people to view the expedition and its underlying purpose in the noblest light possible.

It also explains why native voices are being drowned out in the celebratory din. When our elders speak, they do not disrespect Lewis and Clark. But they do raise basic points that differ from a wholly positive view of the expedition. The elders tell us, first of all, that this was and is our land, the place prepared for us by Coyote, the place where we have lived for a very long time. They tell us that we were and are a sovereign nation. They tell us that we were kind and generous to non-Indian visitors. And the elders tell us that the expedition was part of a long process of unprovoked invasion, the taking of our resources, the stripping of our rights of sovereignty and self-determination, the marginalization of our cultural ways. From the perspective of our elders, the expedition was less an innocent "Corps of Discovery" than a reconnaissance for invasion.

We know this will be a difficult message for some readers to hear. It cannot be squared with a blind celebration of Lewis and Clark. But we know that many people are more interested in understanding the expedition than in simply glorifying it. Many are concerned about the damage the continuing distortion of our past does to all of us, and especially to the countless native children who are exposed every day to a false depiction of their own cultures and histories. Many people are interested in a more realistic assessment of American history, even if it is a less comfortable assessment. To reach that point, we must begin by listening to the voices that have until now been left out.

By presenting the expedition within this larger context, we hope in this book to broaden the national conversation on Lewis and Clark. Most of all, we hope our

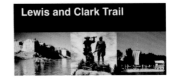

small contribution will help other tribes gain the opportunity to put their own voices forward. Only then will we reach a deeper and more complete understanding of this history.

In telling our own story, our biggest task is to provide readers with a deeper understanding of the cultural and historical landscape Lewis and Clark were traversing as they passed through the mountains and valleys of western Montana in 1805 and 1806.

We must begin by explaining who we are. Non-Indians have often called us Flatheads, a misnomer that took root shortly after Lewis and Clark passed through western Montana in 1805–6. We are also sometimes called the Bitterroot Salish, in reference to part of our homeland, the Bitterroot Valley, south of present-day Missoula, Montana. In our own language, we call ourselves the Séliš (pronounced Séh-lish). *Salish* is the common English rendition of the word, and it is used in most official tribal documents today. We therefore use *Salish* throughout this volume. We are the easternmost tribe of the peoples who makeup the Salish language family, which extends from Montana all the way to the Pacific Coast, generally on the north side of the Columbia River.

The sprawling aboriginal territory of the Salish straddled both sides of the Continental Divide in what is now the state of Montana. About 1750–1800, because of losses from epidemics and pressures from rifle-armed Blackfeet raiders, our people moved their headquarters into the Bitterroot Valley and the western portion of the overall aboriginal territory (see "The Beginning of the Great Changes" in part 2 of this volume). We continued to utilize the plains east of the mountains for hunting and other purposes. In fact, when Lewis and Clark arrived in 1805, the Salish band they encountered was on its way east to hunt buffalo. Today, the Salish people are based on the Flathead Indian Reservation, a 1.2-million-acre area north of Missoula, Montana. The reservation is part of the original homeland of our close relations, the Pend d'Oreille (see "'This Land Was Good'" in part 1 of this volume).

The Flathead Reservation is also home to one band of the Kootenai people, who speak a separate and unrelated language. The Salish-language name for the Kootenai is Sqlsé. They refer to themselves as the Ktunax̣a; the band that lives within the Flathead Reservation is called the Ksanka.

The tribal government of the Flathead Reservation is today known officially as the Confederated Salish and Kootenai Tribes.

In the pages that follow, we have drawn heavily on Salish oral histories, particularly in "The Salish World in 1805," part 1 of this volume. For the specific stories of the encounter with Lewis and Clark in Part 2, we have combined interviews with tribal elders from a variety of written sources compiled by non-Indian researchers over the years with excerpts from our recorded oral histories.

There are not many of the latter. Some elders today say that when they were young, they never once heard the old people talk about Lewis and Clark.[1] Those who do recall some stories say they were few in number and not very long. Although the non-Indian invasion that followed the expedition obviously had a very great effect on the lives and livelihoods of the Salish, the encounter with Lewis and Clark in itself did not occupy a very prominent place in tribal oral tradition. A number of white writers, because of their interest in this subject, relentlessly interviewed Salish and Pend d'Oreille people about the expedition, to the exclusion of issues of far greater significance in tribal history. Few of those early researchers asked the elders much about precontact tribal history, or about the devastation of the Salish world that the expedition set in motion. Despite the limited importance of this encounter within tribal oral tradition, the stories are still remarkable in their detail, and in the way many of those details precisely match the expedition's written journals.[2]

Oral tradition stands at the center of virtually all tribal cultures and histories. Until recently, the stories of traditional tribal elders have been given little weight by most historians. They have been treated as unreliable hearsay, the shifting opinion of biased speakers. Over the past several decades, however, this view has gradually changed, as awareness has grown of the rigorous discipline and accountability surrounding the transmission of oral tradition within many tribal societies.

Among the Salish and Pend d'Oreille, one measure of the reliability of our oral literature can be found in various written and recorded tellings of traditional Coyote stories. The first written record of our oral tradition dates to the mid-nineteenth century, when non-Indian researchers and missionaries, working with native translators, wrote down a number of Coyote stories. In recent decades, we recorded many of those same stories with our elders. Although these tellings are separated by a century of overwhelming upheaval and staggering cultural loss in the Salish community, they are virtually identical in their content and form.[3]

We have been able to ground this history in our own oral tradition because of the existence of tribal cultural institutions that have supported this work for many years. In the 1970s, at the urging of both elders and younger people, the governing council of the Confederated Salish and Kootenai Tribes established culture committees as tribal governmental programs charged with the preservation, protection, and perpetuation of traditional cultures and languages. The Salish-Pend d'Oreille Culture Committee, originally called the Flathead Culture Committee, began its work by simply calling together the most culturally knowledgeable elders and then recording their stories—in the Salish language—on virtually every aspect of tribal culture and history. In the past, elders too often felt exploited and manipulated by non-Indian researchers and scholars, who were often viewed by the elders with some suspicion. The establishment of the culture committees made it possible, for the first time, for elders to be interviewed in their own language by younger tribal members who were fluent in their language and knowledgeable about tribal history and culture. That climate of trust and familiarity prompted the elders to share the histories, the creation stories, the songs—the great oral literature that had been passed down to them from time immemorial. In succeeding years, culture committee staff members painstakingly translated the interviews into English, while others revisited the tapes and transcribed them in the written Salish language, using the International Phonetic Alphabet (see "A Brief Guide to Written Salish" at the end of this volume). Finally, all of this material was computerized, indexed, and organized. The end result—hundreds of audio and video tapes and thousands of pages of transcripts—constitute one of the finest and most extensive tribal archives in the nation. And that archive has provided the core material for this and several other major books now being produced by the Salish-Pend d'Oreille Culture Committee.

This project, then, is the reflection of many years of support for tribal culture committees and a shared sense among tribal government leaders that the preservation and perpetuation of our culture and history is a vital necessity for our survival as a people. We owe much to that institutional stability, made possible by the long, steady support of the Tribal Council of the Confederated Salish and Kootenai Tribes.

Numerous other people outside of the Salish-Pend d'Oreille Culture Committee have also made important

Members of Salish-Pend d'Oreille Elders Cultural Advisory Council, June 2002. Front row, left to right: *Josephine Quequesah, Clara Bourdon, Sophie Haynes, Felicite Sapiel McDonald, Alice Camel, Margaret Finley, Janie Wabaunsee.* Middle row: *Louie Adams, John Stanislaw, Bud Barnaby, Eneas Vanderburg, Noel Pichette, Stephen Smallsalmon.* Back row: *Pat Pierre, Michael Louis Durglo Sr., Octave Finley, Joe Cullooyah.* Missing: *Agnes Pokerjim Paul, Dolly Linsebigler.*

contributions to this project, and they deserve our thanks and praise.

Former culture committee staff member Germaine White served for a time as a tribal spokesperson on matters relating to the Lewis and Clark bicentennial, helped conceive this book and served as an editor, and helped us in our work with the University of Nebraska Press. She also wrote an important grant that enabled us to hire Tony Sandoval and his sons, T.J. and Sam, to create original artwork for this book. The grant also helped with part of the publication costs.

The Tribal Preservation Office helped administer the grant for the original artwork, and special thanks go to Shannon Burke for her after-hours administrative work. Tony Sandoval shared our commitment to express the elders' voices, and he worked tirelessly and uncomplainingly with the Elders Cultural Advisory Council to ensure that his paintings are as accurate as possible. His sons, T.J. and Sam, conceptualized many of the paintings and drew sketches on which they were based.

We owe a dept of gratitude also to Corky Clairmont, Director of the Art Department at Salish Kootenai College and an internationally acclaimed native artist, who generously allowed us to use some of his brilliant multimedia works addressing the Salish encounter with the Lewis and Clark expedition. Thanks also to the Eiteljorg Museum, Indianapolis, and Jennifer McNutt for use of Dirk Bakker's excellent photographs of Corky's work.

Thanks also go to other tribal readers of the draft, including Julie Cajune, Indian Education Coordinator with the Ronan School District and for a time the tribal spokesperson on Lewis and Clark issues; Terry Tanner of the Tribal Wildlands Recreation Program and former culture committee employee; and former culture committee employee Gene Beaverhead.

Doug Allard gave us generous and free access to his outstanding collection of photographs relating to the tribes and the reservation. These images add greatly to this and other culture committee projects. Other photographers and archivists graciously helped us in locating and obtaining copies of images used in this book. We have been grateful, and fortunate, that almost all generously allowed us free use of their photographs. We give our sincere thanks to Kristen Mable, Barry Landau, and Dr. Peter Whiteley at the American Museum of Natural History in New York; the Bitter Root Valley Historical Society and its Executive Director, Helen Bibler; Roger Dunsmore of Missoula; Susan Kooyman of the Glenbow Archives in Calgary, Alberta; David Kingma of the Jseuit Oregon Province Archives at Gonzaga University in Spokane, Washington; Susan Otto at the Milwaukee Public Museum; Lory Morrow, Becca Kohl, and Jennifer Bottomly-O'Looney at the Montana Historical Society in Helena; Steve Jackson at the Museum of the Rockies, Montana State University in Bozeman; Daisy Njoku at the National Anthropological Archives, Smithsonian Institution, Washington DC; Eric Bittner at the Rocky Mountain Region branch of the National Archives in Denver; David Spear, an instructor at Salish Kootenai College; Suzanne Vernon and the Swan Ecosystem Center in Condon, Montana; Jessie Nunn at the University of Montana's K. Ross Toole Archives in Missoula; and Charles Kline of the University of Pennsylvania. Again, our thanks to all.

We are deeply indebted to Gary Dunham, Director of the University of Nebraska Press, who immediately understood what we were trying to do with this book and shared our sense of its importance. Gary made extraordinary efforts to reach out to the tribal community, and when we saw his immediate rapport with the elders we knew we had a rare find. We owe much to his commitment to shepherding the project through the long road toward publication. Other members of Nebraska's extraordinary staff gave us great support throughout the process, in particular Margie Rine, Sandra Johnson, Linnea Frederickson, Debra Turner, Beth Ina, and Ray Boeche. And Sarah Disbrow was all we could have wished for in a copy editor: precise, rigorous, and thorough—yet infinitely flexible and never without a sense of humor. All helped vastly improve this book and make it a reality, while respecting the elders' vision and their ultimate say over all aspects of content and form.

We are also grateful for generous funding from a number of sources. The Montana Lewis and Clark Bicentennial Commission funded artwork and part of the publication cost. The Montana Committee for the Humanities has been a crucial supporter of our work for many years, and they awarded this book their sole subvention grant for 2003. The American Public Land Exchange

Company and Mr. Bruce Bugbee appeared out of the blue to give us important funding and, with the kind approval of Todd Kaplan, also allowed us the use of some of Mr. Kaplan's stunning photographs of the Bitterroot Valley landscape. Special thanks go especially to two foundations who provided substantial funding for publication: the Plum Creek Foundation and Mr. Bob Marcinich, and the Dennis and Phyllis Washington Foundation and Mr. Mike Halligan. Without their collective support, this book would not have made it into print.

One of the most important aspects of the project, the careful review of the book by tribal elders, could not have happened without the cooks who prepared lunches for our meetings. Our thanks go to Dorothy Woodcock, Monique McDonald, and LaMoine Hendrickson.

The Salish People and the Lewis and Clark Expedition is, however, most of all the product of the elders themselves. Not only does this book rest upon the stories and information the elders have generously provided, but it also has been carefully and tirelessly reviewed by them in numerous meetings at the Salish-Pend d'Oreille Longhouse. Following the last chapter, we offer short profiles of elders past and present whose contributions helped make this book a reality, and also their own words on this project and the history it examines.

The Salish elders today are continuing an unbroken chain of oral tradition that was told to them by their elders, who received it from their elders. And that unbroken chain, that oral record of Salish culture and history, reaches back to the ancestors and the earliest beginnings of human history in what is now Montana. In spite of all that has happened over the past two hundred years, our elders have persevered in carrying on our oral tradition, in the simple hope that future generations will in turn pass it on to their children and grandchildren.

In short, the elders are both authors and editors of this book. If it faithfully expresses their voices, it will have succeeded.

SALISH-PEND D'OREILLE CULTURE COMMITTEE
FEBRUARY 2004

Antoine "Tony" Incashola, *Director*

Felicite Sapiel McDonald, *Senior Translator and Advisor*

Michael Louis Durglo Sr., *Indigenous Mapping Project (with Tribal Preservation Department)*

Shirley Trahan, *Salish Language Specialist*

Josephine Quequesah, *Translator*

Chauncey Beaverhead, *Data Entry Technician*

Sadie Peone, *Historical Collections Manager*

Gloria Whitworth, *Office Manager*

Richard Alexander, *Maintenance Technician*

Thompson Smith, *Tribal History & Geography Projects*

Following pages:

The Day Lewis and Clark Came. *Oil painting by Tony Sandoval, 2003.*

Mission Valley & Mission Mountains, 1884.

Bitterroot River near Tmsmɫí (Lolo), 2003.

Josephine Camille & daughter Lucy, 1906.

Tipi rings near 16 Mile Creek, 1940.

Bitterroot River, 2002.

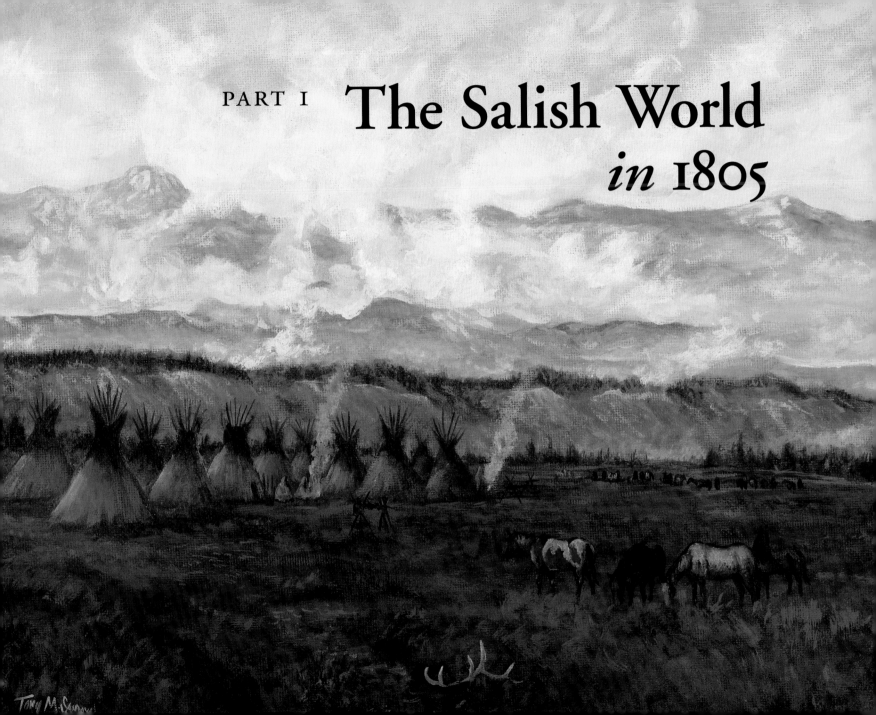

PART I **The Salish World**
in 1805

Łu tsq̓si . . .   A long time ago . . .
neⱡi l es milk̓ʷ ye sⱦúlixʷ   all over this land

u es t̓uk̓ʷ ɫu maliyémistis ɫu sqélixʷ . . .　　　the people's medicine was put here . . .

X̣est! X̣est es ay̓ew̓ti,
x̣est es p̓ox̣ʷtiƚ̓ši ƚu
sxʷsixʷlts ƚu tsq̓si sqélixʷ.

It was good! Their home life was good, they were
growing up in a good way,
the children of the long-ago people.

I xʷukʼʷ ye sʼtulixʷ   The land was clean,

I xʷukʼʷ ye nwíst,   the air was clean,

esya? u x̣e.   everything was good.

— Mitch Smallsalmon, 1978

Coyote *and* the Ice Age

Tribal Creation Stories and Tribal Origins

The traditional oral literature of the Salish and Pend d'Oreille people begins with the *sqʷlllum̓t*—the creation stories, the stories of how the world came to be and of the nature of things in this world. These sacred stories, passed down for thousands of years, were told only during the winter months.*

Many of the stories tell of Snčlé, Coyote, who traveled across the land, killing the *naɫisqélixʷtn*—the people-eaters or monsters. Coyote made the world safe for the people who were yet to come. He prepared the land and made it good. He showed us how to live in a good way, and also how not to live, and the consequences of both good and bad actions.

The stories teach many things: the traditional ways of hunting and fishing; the places used for gathering certain plants for foods and medicines; the clothing; the tools and weapons; the music; the proper ways of child-raising; the relations between men and women; the relations between people of different tribes; the spiritual dimensions of the world; human relations with animals; how things would be in the future; even the sense of humor. All of these things come from the stories of Coyote and the other animal people, of what they did in the time before the beginning of the world as we know it.

All peoples have a literature of creation. But the traditional stories of the Salish and Pend d'Oreille, like those of many other indigenous peoples around the world, are often site-specific. They tell not only of the origin of the world, but also of how deeply the people are tied to this particular place. This is where the people were put and where we were intended to live. It is the land we were entrusted to care for and to pass on to succeeding generations. Coyote prepared the land for us, and he left behind landmarks to remind the people of his deeds. Throughout the immense Salish-Pend d'Oreille aboriginal territory, many of the land formations—even entire valleys, rivers, mountains, and lakes—are tied to these ancient stories of creation and transformation. Many of the traditional placenames, in fact, are derived from the Coyote stories, as we will see in greater detail later in Part I, "A Salish Journey through the Bitterroot Valley."

The legends of Coyote and the other animal people, and the placenames tied to these stories, also tell us something about how long the Salish and Pend d'Oreille

* As readers discuss this book, we ask that the Coyote stories mentioned in these pages be repeated only in the winter.

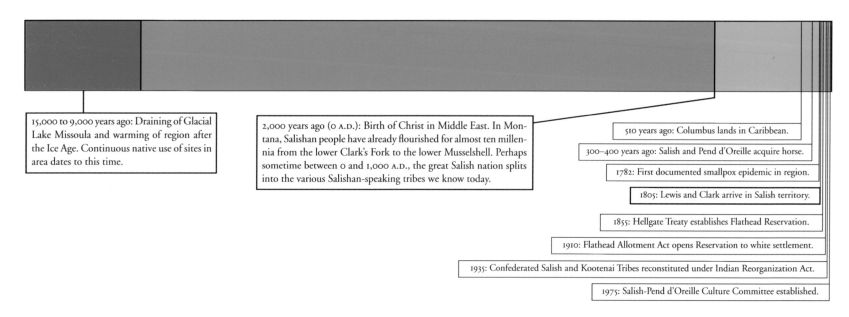

15,000 to 9,000 years ago: Draining of Glacial Lake Missoula and warming of region after the Ice Age. Continuous native use of sites in area dates to this time.

2,000 years ago (0 A.D.): Birth of Christ in Middle East. In Montana, Salishan people have already flourished for almost ten millennia from the lower Clark's Fork to the lower Musselshell. Perhaps sometime between 0 and 1,000 A.D., the great Salish nation splits into the various Salishan-speaking tribes we know today.

510 years ago: Columbus lands in Caribbean.

300–400 years ago: Salish and Pend d'Oreille acquire horse.

1782: First documented smallpox epidemic in region.

1805: Lewis and Clark arrive in Salish territory.

1855: Hellgate Treaty establishes Flathead Reservation.

1910: Flathead Allotment Act opens Reservation to white settlement.

1935: Confederated Salish and Kootenai Tribes reconstituted under Indian Reorganization Act.

1975: Salish-Pend d'Oreille Culture Committee established.

Salish-Pend d'Oreille Timeline: From the Ice Age to the Present

people have been here. They tell us that our tribes, and our ancestors, have inhabited what is now western Montana from the time when the landmarks, the great rocks and hot springs and canyons, were made that way by Snčl̓é. Coyote stories, in short, are both the great spiritual literature of the Salish and Pend d'Oreille people, and also a reflection of the length and depth of the collective tribal memory, which reaches back to the distant beginnings of the people's history.

Indeed, the tenure of the Salish and Pend d'Oreille is so old that in western Montana, the beginnings of human history shade back into a period that we usually consider the province of geologists. In many of the tribal creation stories, we find uncanny parallels with the findings of scientists regarding the end of the last Ice Age. Coyote stories describe the extension of the glaciers

down what is now Flathead Lake, the flooding of western Montana beneath a great lake (what geologists call Glacial Lake Missoula), and the breaking up of the ice dam that contained those waters. The stories tell of the gradual retreat, advance, and then final retreat of the bitter cold weather and the establishment of the seasons and climate we know today, as the Ice Age came to an end. They also describe the disappearance of large animals such as giant beaver and giant bison, and their replacement by the smaller versions of these species. Some of the traditional stories even seem to suggest that our ancestors were already here when the Ice Age began.

Many scholars have long been skeptical of all this, thinking there was little physical evidence that Salish and Pend d'Oreille people had been here that long ago. But tribal and non-Indian archaeologists have now documented sites in places such as Paradise, near the confluence of the Flathead and Clark's Fork rivers—in the very heart of tribal territory—that reflect a continuous occupancy reaching back to the end of the last Ice Age. Others have noted the lithic scatter left along the shoreline of Glacial Lake Missoula, reflecting occupancy of the shoreline before the time the lake repeatedly drained, refilled, and drained again, beginning about 15,000 years ago and ending about 13,000 years ago.[1]

The references to the last Ice Age in Salish-Pend d'Oreille oral traditions reflect a tribal presence in our region over an immense span of time—so immense that it forces us to reconsider what we commonly conceive of as the scope of human history. It compels us to face the depth of misunderstanding that is perpetuated when we are told, over and over again, that the Lewis and Clark expedition marks the beginning of western U.S. history. For in fact, the entire period since 1800 comprises little more than 1 percent of the history of the Salish and Pend d'Oreille people.

We have drawn a rough timeline of Salish-Pend d'Oreille history (see page 8). Readers will note the arrival of Lewis and Clark marked near the far right-hand edge. The time line tells us that the entire period since Columbus arrived in North America—displayed in lightest green at the far right end—constitutes less than 6 percent of the span of Salish-Pend d'Oreille history, using the conservative starting point of about 9,000 years ago. If we were to represent this time line as a single 24-hour day, Lewis and Clark would arrive at about 11:28 p.m.—about half an hour before midnight.

From this broader historical context, we can better understand just how recently and how suddenly the Salish world was transformed by the upheaval associated with non-Indian incursions into tribal territories. And we can better understand why, in the following pages, the past 500 years are condensed into a single story by tribal historians Pete Beaverhead and Mitch Smallsalmon. For the elders, the historical meaning of Lewis and Clark must be understood within the broader context of the sudden, and relatively recent, non-Indian invasion of native North America.

The Big Picture

Tribal Elders on the Sweep of History
from Columbus to Lewis and Clark
to the Allotment Act

In the following accounts, tribal elders Pete Beaverhead, Mitch Smallsalmon, and Sam Resurrection situate the Lewis and Clark expedition within the broad context of tribal history.

These accounts describe a number of specific details relating to the encounter with Lewis and Clark, such as how the Salish decided to welcome the strangers and how they shared robes and food with them. Most of these details are also mentioned in tribal accounts later in this book, and some are also described in the expedition's own journals.

But in the following three passages, the elders also draw the big picture. They integrate the specific history of the Salish encounter with Lewis and Clark within the larger history of the Euro-American invasion of native lands in the Americas. And they also integrate their knowledge of tribal oral histories and the stories they have heard elsewhere of such things as the landing of Columbus (which had been assiduously taught to tribal schoolchildren by Jesuit missionaries).

The following stories, in other words, set Lewis and Clark within the long arc of Indian-white relations be-ginning with the landing of Columbus and continuing through to the General Allotment Act of 1887,[1] after which tribal lands on reservations were broken up by Congress and opened to white settlement. The elders are telling us that these are chapters in the same story. All are examples of the gradual non-Indian invasion of Indian lands and of the arrogance and violence of the Doctrine of Discovery, the claiming of someone else's land, as Mitch Smallsalmon says, merely by planting a "flag in the ground."

"They hadn't seen our land yet, and they had already sold it."

Pete Beaverhead

K̓ʷeṁt łihéʔ ye iʔs meyeʔm.
Then when I thought about it,

K̓ʷeṁt łu k̓ʷłpáʔx̣nten,
Then when I thought about it,

čn nté tl̓ čełl nq̓ʷoqey smx̣ʷop
I think it is about three hundred snows ago,

u č msłnq̓ʷoqey
and four hundred snows ago, and even

čičciʔ.
beyond that time.

U npx̣mú ečx̣ey
And it's like that is when we've reached

łu i tmi.
the end of what is known.

Łu iqs cmeyyeʔ łu
What I am going to tell is what was

in qnqeneʔ,
passed on to me by my paternal

i slsileʔ,
grandmothers, my maternal

i sx̣px̣épeʔ,
grandfathers, and my paternal

in ilaẇiyeʔs,
grandfathers by their great-great-

ṫpṫúpiyeʔs,
grandparents, and their great-

łu es nmicinms....
grandparents. . . .

K̓ʷeṁt tl̓ šeẏ cx̣ʷuy,
Then from there, time passed until it was

ye cčč̓e,
closer to our time now,

u wičis łu suyapi.
and the Indians saw the whiteman.

Nq̓ʷoṅmis łu suyapi,
They felt pity for the white people,

i pqpiq,
because they were white,

u es upupus.
and they had beards.

Ečx̣lús teʔs čłix̣ʷx̣ʷmu
The white men looked as if they were

x̣ʷl̓ is piq i k̓ʷils.
cold because their faces were white and red.

K̓ʷeṁt łu čicntm łu t suyapi
Then, when the Indian people were met by

 k̓ʷ ƛ̓e cnt̓eʔešlš ƚu suyapi,
k̓ʷemt x̌ʷpx̌ʷépis ƚu ep spum ƚu sičm,
še k̓ʷƚsuxʷmeʔis l šeẏ
u qs ƚaqqí.
Cuti ƚu ilmíx̌ʷm,
"N̓em x̌ʷpx̌ʷépntp ci sičm, ci ep spum
m l šeẏ m ƚaqq.
X̌ʷa es siyuẏti."
Es nte es siyuẏti,
u i pqpiqs.
Tl̓ šeẏ es ctax̌ʷllu cx̌ʷuy u miyip
epƚ nččx̌ʷčx̌ʷepletn ƚu suyapi.
Łu qs cníʔek̓ʷ
l ʔes šʔit qs cníʔek̓ʷmi ƚu suyapi
u ƛ̓e qe tumistmƚlt
ƚu qe st̓úlixʷ ƚu l amotqn.
Cuys,
"Q̓ʷu aqs x̌ʷičštm t ƛ̓iyéʔ
čiqs ƛ̓emí t st̓úlixʷ."
K̓ʷemt cuys
ƚu amotqis, ƚu *king*,
"N̓em aqƚ st̓úlixʷ."
K̓ʷemt ƚi i, i čẏú qe es wičƚlt ƚu qe st̓úlixʷ
u ƛ̓e qe tumistmƚlt.

K̓ʷemt cn̓tešlš
u nšt̓ulexʷm
t sččacé.

U k̓ʷemt x̌ʷa ečx̌ey qe k̓ʷƚ̓x̌ʷuʔupčm.

the whitemen (because they had already landed),
the Indian people then spread out their
fur blankets and motioned to the white
men to sit on the blankets.
Their chief told them,
"Spread out the fur blankets
so that the white men can sit on them.
Maybe they are cold."
The Indian people thought the white men were cold
because they were white-faced.
From that time on, it became known
that the white people had laws.
Right then, when the white men were to
come across the ocean for the first time, our
land had already been sold by them to the
government, their king or leader.
The whiteman told their leader,
"You give me a ship to go across
to look for some land."
He told
his leader, his king,
"It will be your land."
They hadn't even seen our land yet
and they had already sold it.

The whiteman crossed and landed,
and he stuck
a flag and pole in the ground.

And then it's like they beat us out of our land.

13

Łu es š?í sqélixʷ wičis,
kʷeṁt kʷnkʷenštm t sq̓l̓q̓l̓é
t scłkʷłikʷ.
Šeẏ łu nx̣eselsmis, lemtmis,
łu t sqélixʷ.
Kʷeṁt č šeẏ u qe nunnx̣ʷene?.

Kʷeṁt es mi-i-i-ilkʷ yetłx̣ʷa ye st̓úlixʷ,
qe st̓úlixʷ, ye es čsunk̓ʷ,
u ċx̣eẏ t lčntes x̣ʷl̓ qe nplé.
Qe k̓ʷłqeyx̣ʷłlt łu pn tl̓ qe snlclci?tn.
U qe cułlt łu t suyapi,
"Ihé? łu aqs sqlixʷúlexʷ.
Aqł nlci?tn."
U qe eł łsx̣ʷsux̣ʷmešls
tes heheṅmłʔu acre,
t qeq st̓úlixʷ, t qeqł čmšté.
Qe cułls, "Ihé? łu aqł čmšté,
aqł st̓úlixʷ."
Kʷeṁt nx̣ʷʔit, če kʷtnúlexʷ
łu sm?awlexʷ
u eł k̓ʷul̓is
łu t suyapi
u cnpilš
u qe piṅmłlt.
Unexʷ.
Č qeqs šimi ci eighty acres,
qeqs nlci?tn.
Hoy čtaxʷlle n?eysis łu t suyapi,
łu st̓l̓túlixʷ—qe tumistmntm
u put u qes miš. . . .

The first Indians they saw,
the whites showed them necklaces
that had been strung.
The people liked them and were glad to
get them. Then from that we believed
and trusted them.

Today, this land a-a-a-all over,
our land, this island—
today, the whiteman has tied it up for us.
They blocked us out of our homelands.
And the whiteman told us,
"This is to be your Indian land, your Reservation.
It is where you will live."
Then they set it up, surveyed it
in 80 acres, to be our land, to be for our
own, for each of us to possess individually.
We were told, "This is here is to be your
own, to own, your land."
It was a vast area of land, and there was
a lot left over after they gave us those pieces,
and the white people arranged it so that we
sold the land; we sold it, and it was bought
by the whiteman, and they came in and
crowded us out.
It is the truth.
All we got was that eighty acres,
for our place to live.
That's when the whiteman began buying it,
all the lands—we sold it,
and now it is almost all gone. . . .

"When he got off his ship he put his flag in the ground, just like he put a brand on this land."

Mitch Smallsalmon

Ḱeṁt l šeẏ u es čšín,	Then time went by,
u ɫu x̣ʷa l čeṅ u ax̣ey	and it came to pass
u ɫu es šʔí suyá cx̣ʷuy,	that the first whiteman came here,
ɫu es custm *Columbus.*	the one who is called Columbus.
Ḱeṁt ɫu cnṫešlš,	When he came across
u wičis ye sṫúlixʷ,	and saw this land,
ṫipncú ɫu tɬ ƛiyéʔs	he got off his ship,
u nšṫulexʷis ɫu sccacé.	and he put his flag in the ground.
Ċx̣ey es lemti,	I guess same as saying he was glad,
es lemti tixʷ sṫúlixʷ.	glad to acquire some land.
U wičis, we wičis ye sqélixʷ,	He did see the Indians standing in
tutupiyeẇt, es tʔaccx̣.	groups all staring at him.
Ḱeṁt ta es misten, ta ciqs cu ɫu,	But I don't know, I'm not going to
ɫu l šeẏ u ecx̣eẏ ɫu sck̓ʷɫpaʔx̣s ɫu suyá.	say what was on the white people's
Ḱeṁt ck̓ʷɫčí	minds. Then just as soon as he arrived
u ƛe, ƛe p̓ix̣is	here, it was just like he put a brand on
ye sṫúlixʷ.	this land.
ƛe wičm t qs sṫúlixʷs,	He found some land for himself,
u ta x̣ʷa es k̓ʷestc ci,	but I don't think he carried any kind
cniɫc snččx̣ʷeples.	of important papers about laws.
Łu ċx̣ey qs nčmeɫxʷ	And to come here and take away
ye t qe sqélixʷ, k̓ʷ ɫu t sṫúlixʷ,	and claim our Indian land—
ċx̣eẏ ta es čsewpleʔís	he didn't even have permission
čmi neɫí.	from anyone to take our land.
Ḱeṁt č̓ snččx̣ʷepletis	But I guess they thought they'd just
u tk̓ʷuntes.	go ahead and use their own laws.

The previous accounts, told by Mitch Smallsalmon and Pete Beaverhead, were recorded during the 1970s. The following account, a letter addressed to the commissioner of Indian affairs in Washington DC was dictated in 1913 by Salish elder Sam Resurrection, and translated and written down by younger tribal members who had received some schooling. The letter is reproduced here just as it was typed out, and we must bear in mind that it may not exactly express what Mr. Resurrection said in Salish. Despite these problems of translation and transcription, this document sets the tribal encounter with Lewis and Clark into the same context, the same flow of history, the same long story of the non-Indian taking of native lands and resources as the accounts provided by Mitch Smallsalmon and Pete Beaverhead six decades later. The following letter, in short, clearly shows that this perspective has long been the predominant tribal understanding of this event.

"Three Eagle . . . order[ed that] these strange people were not to be mistreated or harmed."

Sam Resurrection

Arlee, Montana, 1913.

Twenty-six men that had been president in the U.S. We all Indian tribe are very sorry for we have lost our power in everything; None of these twenty-six presidents did anything good for us North American Indians. . . .

I am the Celish Indian. I am an American. . . .

This is made up by Sam Resurrection, a good, worthy, prominent Flathead Indian.

Born in Stevensville, Montana, January 20th 1860, in the beautiful country of Stevensville, about 60 miles from Jocko, Montana.

Was once the Flathead home. Mr. Sam Resurrection and his people lived there for a long time. They moved northward to Jocko, Montana, known today as the Reservation of the Flathead Indians.

Sam Resurrection is a good, honest man, is always working for his people. He is very sorrowful now for the Whites are not treating the Flathead Indians right.

I will kindly remind you whites that this continent of North America, centuries ago early belong to the red men of the continent. It is fully understood this continent and whatsoever is created by the Almighty, it is well known to all. That only the Indians and no other human race used to dwell on this continent, and so it could be easily seen and clearly understood that this continent from coast to coast once belonged to the Indians. Only Christopher Columbus sailed August 3rd, 1492, landed in America October 12, 1492, 421 years ago, so he was the first who made a footprint on this continent of North America, and he was the first white man to be seen by the Indians. 107 years ago at Rossel Hole, Lewis and Clark's parties was met by the Indians, the Selish of Flathead, now called, that was the first whites to be seen by the Indians of the Flathead tribe. The Flathead Chief of the Selish tribe was Mr. Three Eagle. He gave an order to his tribe as these strange people were seen, that they were not to be mistreated or harmed and was always to have respect for them. And so from that time we Selish always kept the work of the great Chief Three Eagle.

Governor Stevens' treaty, the year of 1855, July 16th at Hell Gate, Governor Stevens informed the Selish, upper Pondera and Kooteanies that he was sent under the Act of the Department to make a Reservation for the said tribe, agrees that the Reservation and the firm solid boundaries and the boundary will be completed, it will be firm and it will last until the last Indian of said tribe passes away and the hunting grounds are to be freely opened for the said tribe. The head Chief of the Salish was Victor, and of the Ponderas, Alexander and of the Kootanies Michel, so those three Chiefs gladly agreed and the treaty was completed by Governor Stevens and since either we kept and hold onto their treaty and it is surprising to see that our Reservation thrown open without our consent and it has brought to us a great grief unto this present date and now moreover, the rights of our men are killed by the whites on our hunting grounds. All tribe treaty in Montana with Governor Stevens at Yellow river 1855 in Fall. The treaty of Governor Stevens was with the Salish, Pondaries, Blackfeet, Cheyenne Snakes, and the Nezperz. He informed the said tribes that fighting and war between themselves ought to be brought to an end and not be enemies to

each other but to be always friendly. They kindly took the work of Governor Stevens and since then they were always friendly.

Treaty of Garfield and Selish 40 years ago he inquired how the treaty was made with Governor Stevens. Chief Charlos was then the Head Chief of the Selish and he told him that a Reservation was made for the Indians to dwell in it as long as the tribe shall last, so then Garfield made a treaty alike that of Governor Stevens'. Twenty-two (22) years ago, General H. B. C. Carrington, arrived in the Bitter Root valley, and imprisoned Charlo, the Selish Chief. He said that he was sent under the Act of the Department to remove the Selish from the Bitter Root valley into the Reservation, now called the Flathead Reservation. That if they agreed that this Reservation, as mentioned before, was to have firm boundary lines and that they were never to be disturbed, Charlo and his band gladly removed into the Flathead Reservation, according to the promise of H. B. Carrington, 35 years ago.

The Nezperz got into a war with the whites. During that time the whites of the Bitter Root valley asked for help of the Flathead against the Nezperz and so the Flathead said their lives and stand for the whites to see that no harm or bloodshed was done in the Bitter Root valley by the Nezperz.

We Flathead are always friendly and the best of respect to the whites. A year after this war, help was again asked for by the whites of the Flathead, and some of them joined with the soldiers, going up the Bitter Root valley on a look-out for the Nezperz. I went to Washington D.C. two times to see the President of the United States, and I never saw him. I tried my best to see him. I went to the White House twice and I found out all of the Indian tribes do not see the President and from then on I have been very sorry for not seeing the President. It is now four years ago I saw Joe Dixon on March 23rd, and I talked with him. I told him who told you to open the Flathead Reservation. Asked him, Joe Dixon, who is the boss of all the Indians? Where did he have treaty with the Selish Indians? He answered and said "I don't know". I told Joe Dixon "I am glad we meet together" and I asked him all the questions and he did not answer any of them. I said "Joe Dixon, you better stop your lying about the Flathead Reservation". I came back to the Flathead Indians and we had council and I told them about the meeting with Joe Dixon. All my people were glad to hear my news. Of course it is Joe Dixon who spoiled everything for us Selish Indians.

All you white people and all Indians know that this continent of North America is made for every white and every Indian of every nation.

It is now seven years, I have been reminding you white people of everything. 29 years ago 1884 four of our Indians were killed by the whites for hunting wild animals, two men and two women. Four years ago in 1909 four Indians were killed on their hunting ground, three men and one boy. You whites don't think of this.

Mr. Sam Resurrection is very sorry for the whites had killed these eight Indians on their hunting trip for not doing any harm to any white. I have never done any wrong thing with the whites nor to Indians. Never did

steal nor killed any one in my life time. I take this continent for my Father and Mother. I know this continent is our strength for all American Indians.

Salish encampment, probably near Arlee, c. 1915.

SAM RESURRECTION.
ARLEE, MONTANA.

"This Land Was Good"

The Traditional Cycle of Life

In the preceding pages, Pete Beaverhead, Mitch Small-salmon, and Sam Resurrection set the Lewis and Clark expedition within the context of the overall history of non-Indian incursions into tribal territories. And as we have seen, even that five-hundred-year history is only the most recent period of a tribal history that reaches back to the Ice Age, a history that shades back into the spiritual stories of creation and the deeds of Coyote and the other animal-people.

The elders tell that long ago, when the ancestors first lived upon this land, there was a single Salishan nation, which spoke one language. As the tribe increased in population, the people dispersed into numerous smaller groups, eventually forming the various Salishan tribes we know today—Salish, Pend d'Oreille, Spokane, Colville, Coeur d'Alene, Okanagan, and others, each with its own dialect, its own specific culture, and its own territory. The Salish, as mentioned in the introduction, are the easternmost of this string of Salish-speaking tribes which together extend from Montana westward across Washington and British Columbia north of the Columbia River, all the way to the Pacific Coast.[1] Linguists estimate that the Salishan bands dispersed and began to develop their distinct dialects thousands of years ago.[2]

The story of the great Salish Nation and its dispersal further underscores the sheer length of tribal history. In the few pages we have here, we cannot possibly retrace the history of the millennia that preceded Lewis and Clark. But in our efforts to convey more fully the depth of tribal history, and the recentness of the Salish-Pend d'Oreille encounter with non-Indians, it is also necessary to understand something of the depth of the tribal relationship with this place—with the land itself, the mountains and valleys, the rivers and lakes, the plants and animals of this vast tribal territory.

The aboriginal lands of the Salish and Pend d'Oreille reached across all of western Montana and considerable ground east of the mountains, north into what is now Canada, west into northern Idaho and eastern Washington, and south into Wyoming. The five or six main bands of the Salish proper were based at winter camps spread between the Bitterroot Valley and Three Forks.

Geographically, culturally, and linguistically, the Pend d'Oreille are the most closely related tribe to the Salish proper. Pend d'Oreille is a French term referring to something hanging from the ear, in reference to the shell earrings the people traditionally wear. Our own tribal name is Qlispé, which has been anglicized as Kalispel. The band of Pend d'Oreille that lived in the

Flathead Lake area and the Mission Valley was called Słq̓tk̓ʷmsčiṅt (People Living along the Shore of the Broad Water, in reference to Čłq̓étk̓ʷ, meaning Broad Water, the name for Flathead Lake). The dialects spoken by the Salish and Pend d'Oreille differ in only minor ways. The Pend d'Oreille lived in a number of bands throughout the drainage systems of the Flathead, Clark's Fork, and Pend d'Oreille rivers in western Montana, northern Idaho, and eastern Washington. Non-Indians have therefore often referred to the "Upper" and "Lower" Pend d'Oreille. The Lower Pend d'Oreille are more commonly known as the Kalispel.

A related band, the Salishan Tuṅáx̣n, lived east of the Continental Divide, and they and the Pend d'Oreille utilized the plains, the Sweetgrass Hills, and adjoining areas for hunting and other purposes.

For millennia, Salish-speaking peoples traveled this enormous area by foot and canoe, visiting and trading with each other, following a seasonal cycle of life and expertly gathering what we needed of the earth's bounty: bitterroots, camas, buffalo, elk, deer, a wide range of fish, a great variety of berries, and dozens of other foods and medicines. The Creator gave our people a rich land to care for and a varied and consequently stable supply of foods, medicines, and all materials necessary for a comfortable life:

Unidentified Salish man, c. 1908.

Nełi łu tsq̓si	Of course, long ago
łiʔe sqélixʷ	the Indian people
łu es xʷlxʷílt	who were living
l milk̓ʷ u esnpyélsi. . . .	were happy all the time. . . .
Ta ma l šeẏ u ec̓x̣ey	You know, that's how things were
łu sqélixʷ łu tsq̓si.	for the Indians long ago.
Esyaʔ łiʔe xʷixʷeẏuł,	All the animals were here,
xʷʔit łu xʷixʷeẏuł.	many animals.
X̌ʷʔít łu t ʔe steṁ	Plenty of everything,
u łiʔe st̓úlixʷ i x̣est	and this land was good.
u łiʔe sx̣aap i xʷuk̓ʷ.	And the air here was clean.

Mitch Smallsalmon[3]

The members of the Lewis and Clark expedition remarked at length on the abundant resources and sheer beauty of the mountains and valleys of the Salish homeland—the "noble streams" of "pure and ice-cold water," the "handsom tall strait pine," the profuse numbers of beaver and in certain areas of other game, the astonishing quantities of berries, roots, and other edible plants. They found this varied landscape perhaps the most dazzling of their entire journey. All the journals repeatedly note the fine appearance of the land, from the "fine pleasant bottoms" of the Smith River to the "beautiful valley" at the Three Forks of the Missouri, from "the extensive beautiful level plains and prairies" along the Clark's Fork near Missoula to the "handsome" country along almost the entire length of the "very beautiful" Blackfoot River. And of course, there was the Bitterroot Valley itself—Clark described it as an idyllic place, a "Vally which we found more bountifully versified with Small open plains covered with a great variety of Sweet cented plants, flowers & grass." And Lewis wrote of its amazing number and variety of birds and plants, and its teeming deer. The journalists also comment at times on scarcity in certain areas, but in general they were stunned by the abundance and quality of the plants and animals in Salish territory—beaver sunning themselves along the banks of the Jefferson River, the "finest currants" they had ever eaten, immense fields of camas bulbs and great thickets of chokecherries, and at places like Three Forks and Lolo and the Dearborn River, a great number of deer and other game.[4]

But how much more astonished would the expedition members have been by this beauty and abundance if they had known how long tribal people had lived here—that this was in fact a place occupied and managed by people far longer than the continent of Europe? For the Salish world was indeed shaped by the people who inhabited it, much as Philadelphia or Washington DC were shaped by their inhabitants. But we shaped our world in ways less obvious and less intrusive than did the agricultural and urban societies to which the expedition members belonged, which exerted more direct control over the plants and animals they relied upon for food. Despite their continual encounters with Indian peoples, Lewis and Clark, like most non-Indians of their time, thought of western North America as a "virgin wilderness." They observed native peoples and native ways of life, and they described the natural world inhabited by Indian people. But Lewis and Clark rarely, if ever, perceived the complex interrelationships between native peoples and native environments. Like other early non-Indian visitors, Lewis and Clark did not realize that the tribes were practicing one of the most sustainable ways of life the world has ever known. Unaware of the length and depth of tribal history, they did not understand that what they saw in western Montana in 1805 was not the product of human absence, but the product of human presence—or more precisely, a particular kind of human presence, a particular cultural relationship to the land, a particular way of life.

Many early non-Indian accounts, including parts of the Lewis and Clark journals, depicted tribal cultures here and elsewhere as a random, even desperate "chase" for food. But in fact, our ancestors enjoyed a way of life of remarkable stability and dependable sustenance. We moved across the land in regular seasonal patterns timed with the fluctuating supplies of plants and animals upon which we relied for food. Our ways of hunting, of fishing, and of gathering plants were based on a profound relationship with this place, on a detailed and precise knowledge—gained through thousands of years of living in one place—of the land's short and long cycles of scarcity and abundance.

Salish and Pend d'Oreille culture, including its technology, was centered on a relationship of respect with all creatures. Almost every elder speaks of how, long ago, one of the central values of the traditional way of life was to waste nothing and to take only what was needed. The elders most often speak of avoiding waste in relation to animals that were killed; by not wasting anything, the people showed their respect for the animal, the one who gave its life so that the people might live. This same ethic also held true for plants, for berries, "for anything else they gathered or killed," as Pete Beaverhead said. The commitment to avoiding waste helped ensure that the plants and animals we depend upon would be sustained for the generations to come. And so the people were never interested in developing the capacity—or the technology—to take or harvest huge surpluses.

The Salish and Pend d'Oreille, and their tribal homelands, were parts of a larger intertribal world, an interlocking system of nations and cultures. Tribes and bands of varying sizes occupied specific, if overlapping, territories. In the entire region, none of the tribes practiced agriculture to meet their subsistence needs, but they did develop regular relationships of trade and exchange with each other. Each relied primarily on the foods that were abundant in that particular area— those foods that were given to each particular people

for their sustenance and their survival. Foods or materials found in great abundance or high quality in the territory of one tribe would be exchanged with "specialties" from other tribes and other places. When the Salish or Pend d'Oreille traveled west, for example, we might trade our camas or finely tanned deer hides for the dried salmon of the Okanagan or Spokane. Sometimes people would exchange goods through formal intertribal gatherings and gift-giving ceremonies. At other times, then as now, they would simply engage in informal gift-giving or trading and bartering between individuals or families. So, while the tribes were largely self-sufficient, they aided and supported each other through these systems of exchange.

The intertribal world that emerged after the dispersal of the great Salish nation was not a world fixed in stone, nor a world without historical change. People constantly made innovations. But our elders have said that the fundamental basis of our way of life remained essentially stable until the great changes of the past five centuries. Indeed, the disruptions and losses of those more recent centuries have undoubtedly erased from our oral traditions knowledge of some of our earlier history. But we know that there was also great stability in our relations with this land, with the plants and animals, and with our neighboring tribes before the arrival of horses and European diseases. Around the world, countless nations and empires rose and fell during that time. But the *sqélix*ʷ—the people—respecting the earth and living within its limits, continued and flourished.

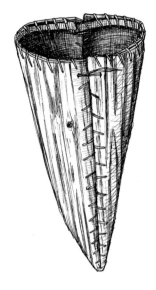

Cedar bark basket.
Drawing by Sam Sandoval. (CSKT).

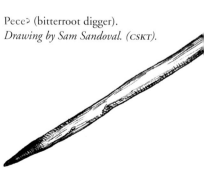

Peceʔ (bitterroot digger).
Drawing by Sam Sandoval. (CSKT).

The Seasonal Cycle of Life

The cycle of the seasons, our movement through the different times of year gathering the traditional foods, begins in the spring. As the elders have told us, "This is the way it is with the Indian people":

N̓e tma łu tsq̓si	You know, a long time ago,
l še u ec̓x̣ey	this is the way it is
łu sqélixʷ.	with the Indian people.
Ye sp̓eλ̓m, ye sx̣ʷeʔli,	The bitterroot, the camas,
ye seč	wild onion,
ci esyaʔ—	and everything else—
u es k̓ʷl tk̓ʷélixʷ łu sqélixʷ	the Indian people are gathering and storing
łu x̣ʷl̓ n̓e ʔistč.	for the winter months ahead.

Pete Woodcock[5]

K̓ʷem̓t n̓e ci eł nk̓ʷu spq̓niʔ	Then the following month,
še λ̓e es t̓ixʷllm.	they do something different.
T̓ʔe stem̓ łu eł es k̓ʷul̓lm.	They are working on something.
Šey̓ łu c̓x̣ey t̓ʔes	Things are rotating, going in a circle all the
šlčmncuti ye sp̓iqałq, u	time, like the berries or things you pick, the
ye scx̣ect,	roots and things you dig,
u y̓e sqq̓m̓e,	and the fishing,
u y̓e sčłip.	and the hunting.
L milk̓ʷ u es q̓ʷápmi,	They are constantly moving,
l milk̓ʷ u es t̓ixʷm.	gathering things all the time.

Pete Beaverhead[6]

When we begin to see the blossoms of the sy̓ey̓eʔ (juneberry) we know the bitterroot is ready. A woman is chosen to sxʷčtim (watch over the bitterroot grounds) to see when it is ready. At the right time, the people come together for the bitterroot ceremony, giving thanks to the bitterroot, "our visitor," the first major food to come out after the long winter. The people harvest just enough for the ceremony, in which we give thanks for all the foods the Creator provides, and for our lives, our survival for another year. After the ceremony, families and groups go out to dig bitterroot in great quantities. As we do for all the other foods—roots, berries, meat—we dry them and store them for our supply throughout the year.

The great bitterroot grounds of the Salish and Pend d'Oreille were scattered across many parts of our aboriginal territories. Many of these places are still used today. One of the most important was Nɫʔaycčstm (Place of the Small Bull Trout), the area around the city of Missoula, Montana. Large areas along Ntx̣ʷétkʷ (the Flathead River) are rich in bitterroot. Lewis and Clark, and most subsequent non-Indian visitors, were little aware of the quantities of bitterroot to be found in these places, or of its importance as a staple that Indian people had harvested sustainably for millennia.

Around the same time of year, the people would hunt smčeč (ground hogs). They were not a staple, but they were valued for food and for their rich fat and oil, which was used for hair grease, among other things. Just north of Čp̓úƛ̓us (Florence), on the east side of the Bitterroot River, is a place called Ep Smčeč (It Has Ground-

hogs). Non-Indians gave it an equivalent name, Woodchuck Creek.

By the end of May or the beginning of June, the bitterroot is close to blooming and can no longer be peeled easily. The next major food, camas, is then ready to be dug. In the many wet prairies and valley bottoms across Salish and Pend d'Oreille territory, vast fields of delicate camas blossoms came into bloom—so many that they appeared to be shimmering blue lakes. The journals of the Lewis and Clark expedition repeatedly mention many of the camas grounds and their value to Indian people throughout the region. Places like Qaɫsá or Epɫ ítx̣ʷeʔ, in the Potomac Valley, were so rich in camas that people from many tribes came there and shared in the bounty.

Łu t qʷoyʔe c̓x̌ey cwič̓tn łu ilmilkʷ
łu isnkʷsqelixʷ,
tma łiʔe qepc x̣ʷa put čen łu spʔniʔ,
še tixʷntm łu qs cʔiʔitis.
Łu tin px̣ʷp̓x̣ʷot x̌eʔect łu t sp̓ełm. . . .
Wis x̌eʔect łu t sp̓ełm
kʷem̓t čtax̣ʷlle x̌eʔect łu t, łu t sx̣ʷeʔli. . . .
seč . . . qł nmełmn
łu l sqʷoleʔeps.
K̓ʷem̓t tiʔixʷis łiʔe qʔes custm
šaw̓tmqn, y̓e Snč̓l̓e q̓ʷomqeys.

What I have seen when I was growing up
was my fellow Indian people,
during some month in the spring,
starting to gather their food.
My parents would dig bitterroot. . . .
After they were done digging bitterroot
then they would start to dig camas. . . .
onions . . . to be a mixture
in their camas baking.
Then they would pick what we call
šaw̓tmqn (tree moss), this Coyote's hair.

Pete Woodcock[7]

Far left: Sp̓ełm (bitterroot).
Drawing by Sam Sandoval. (CSKT).

Left: *Elisepé (Elizabeth Hammer)
and boy with* sp̓ełm, *1940.*

It takes the work of many people over many days to dig enough of the single, deeply buried camas bulbs, and then to bake them in the traditional pits. All of this has to be done carefully, and in the right way— spiritually as well as physically—or the camas will not come out right. When properly baked, camas undergoes a chemical transformation from an inedible bulb to a delicious, sweet source of carbohydrate nutrition.

So important is camas in the traditional way of life that it plays a central role in some of the creation stories. For example, there is a place west of Flathead Lake, near Lonepine, Montana, a place the Salish and Pend d'Oreille call Sqʷl̓eps Snč̓l̓e (Place Where Coyote Baked His Camas). The Kootenai name for this place has the same meaning. Sqʷl̓eps Snč̓l̓e is a twenty-foot-high mound rising out of a low flat along a creek, in an area that has always been important for gathering camas. Like unnumbered tribal people over the millennia,

Pend d'Oreille elder John Peter Paul (1909–2001), when he was a boy, camped there with his mother to gather camas and bitterroot. John told of how, at the beginning, Coyote was making the bed for a river leading all the way from the lower country up toward Flathead Lake, so that salmon would come up there and be food for the people. As Coyote dug the course for this river, he created the Big Draw, an enormous deep valley reaching from the Lonepine-Niarada area toward Sqʷʔeʔ (Corner of the Lake, known in English as Elmo), on the west side of Flathead Lake. But Coyote also wanted to marry one of the women living in the Pend d'Oreille village near Sqʷʔeʔ. In preparation to marry her he had dug some camas and began cooking them in the big mound near Lonepine. But then the woman turned Coyote down. Coyote was mad. He quit building the river passage, leaving in place a big hill separating the Big Draw from Elmo, and salmon never reached Flathead Lake.

Coyote left the area and forgot about his camas. So, to this day, Coyote's camas-baking mound—Sqʷłeps Snčłé—remains where he left it.[8]

At this same time of year—May and June—the sap runs in the trees, and that sap, in the inner cambium layer of the bark, was also a food harvested by the Salish as a sweet, sticky treat. The favorite trees were sʔatqʷłp (ponderosa pine), mulš (cottonwood), and qʷqʷliʔt (lodgepole pine). The people would pry large slabs of bark from the big, healthy trees, taking care not to girdle or harm them. And to this day, wherever you find trees of great size in western Montana, you may see that some old giants bear a semicircular scar on one side. Those great trees were once commonplace throughout the aboriginal territory of the Salish, before most of them were felled by loggers. The surviving scarred trees are part of the historical and cultural landscape of the sqélixʷ.

By the time the people were digging camas and stripping bark from the ancient trees, the creek sides and thickets were scented with wild rose, and the Salish knew that the delicate pink blossoms were a sign that on the prairies east of the mountains, the buffalo were fat:

Łu tsq̓si, łu es custm wiqłčeʔ,	A long time ago, what is called wiqłčeʔ
łu l sʔánłq—	—the summer hunt—
put čʔékʷ łu xʷyé,	just when the wild roses bloom,
še im̓š łu p̓x̣ʷp̓x̣ʷot	our parents and elders
t čłčewšlš,	moved to the plains country,
es tixʷcní t q̓ʷeyq̓ʷay.	to harvest buffalo.
Še put čeyʔiʔilš,	Towards fall,
še eł ctk̓ʷk̓ʷelp.	they would move back home.
Eł im̓š—	Then they move back again—
es custm es m̓šl̓wis.	this is called es m̓šl̓wis—moving from
Put qepc,	camp to camp. When spring came,
še eł ctk̓ʷk̓ʷelp.	they moved back home again.
Łu qe p̓x̣ʷp̓x̣ʷot, łu qe x̣ʷlčmussn.	These were our parents, our ancestors.

Mose Chouteh[9]

Until the 1700s, when the Salish relocated the winter camps to the western portion of our overall territory, most of the tribe lived for most of the year in the buffalo country east of the Continental Divide. We often hunted using the buffalo jumps, including one near the Madison River and one near Great Falls. But even after our people moved the main camps west of the Continental Divide, we continued to rely on the buffalo. In June, Salish hunting parties would begin the journey east across the mountains for the summer hunt. Some people would stay behind to continue baking the camas and to gather other important early summer foods, including sɫaq (serviceberries). These berries were picked in great quantities, dried and stored, and then added to many foods throughout the year. The rest of the tribe would go on ahead, crossing the Clark's Fork and other rivers with "bull boats"—rafts constructed from tipis—and then climbing up the long trails through one of the numerous passes the people used to cross the mountains and continuing out onto the plains to the vast herds that sustained the tribe.

Until buffalo became scarcer, the people usually returned home during summer or early fall. We would conduct another buffalo hunt in the late fall or winter (emšlwis—winter hunt), when the thick fur would make for warm robes. In later times, some parties would stay through the winter on the plains. We relied on medicine men to help the people locate the increasingly scarce buffalo and, at times, to break the bitter cold of plains winters when the very survival of the camp was threatened.

Top: *Cecille Kaiser and Anye Antoine with bags of camas, 1934.*

Bottom: *Agnes Vanderburg peeling bark, Seeley Lake area, c. 1970.*

27

Paul Antoine braiding bison hair rope, 1934.

It is difficult to find an account of buffalo hunting and the use of the buffalo by the elders that does not discuss the lack of waste. There are names in the Salish language for all of the cuts of meat and for all the inside parts of the buffalo. When the hunters went out, they would be followed by the best skinners in the tribe, and when the meat was brought back to camp, the women would have the dry meat racks ready. They would work day and night for several days until all of the buffalo were taken care of. Ribs were used for hide scrapers, hoofs for the meat inside, bones for marrow to use as rifle oil, hair braided for ropes, thick neck hide for ropes and water-tight buckets, hollowed horns for holding gunpowder, sinew for extremely strong thread. The great quantities of meat that were harvested were dried, pounded, packed in parfleches, and taken back west of the mountains. This was also the way of processing meat from deer and elk that we hunted west of the Continental Divide.

When the parfleches were full, the women would inform the chiefs that they should stop hunting so that no buffalo would be wasted. The chiefs would then announce that they would be moving back to the west the next day.

The buffalo hides were also highly prized and Salish and Pend d'Oreille people were and are known for their fine hide work. Some hides would be tanned east of the mountains, while others would be brought back as rawhide and tanned later. Summer hides, which were lighter and easier to work than winter hides, were used for clothing and tipis. Tipi construction was an impor-

tant and difficult art that required great skill and care, and it was conducted in a disciplined way under the supervision of an appointed woman. Tipis were also sometimes made from elk, whose hides were easier to work and lighter for transport than those of buffalo.

For the Salish, as for most people around the world, midsummer has always been a time of relaxation, of visiting, of dressing in our finest clothing and celebrating life, of gathering family, and of renewing friendships. Although the celebrations, or "powwows" as we know them today, have been practiced by the Salish and Pend d'Oreille people for little more than a century, many of the dances and songs originated in tribal gatherings that reach back to time immemorial. And stickgames—the traditional gambling games that are played all through the night at the summer celebrations and through most of the rest of the year—have been played by the tribes of our region for a very long time.

Midsummer is also the time when *st̓šá* (huckleberries) are ready to be gathered. Salish and Pend d'Oreille families and larger groups travel to many favorite places throughout the mountains, camping and harvesting great quantities of the berries. Like other major foods, *st̓šá* were dried and stored for use throughout the winter months. (Today, many of us keep our huckleberries in the freezer.)

Throughout the year—at bitterroot and camas-digging camps, at hunting and berry picking camps, or while in the winter camps—Salish and Pend d'Oreille people also fished. Although fish were not the main part of the traditional diet, they have always been im-

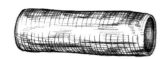

Stickgame bones.
Drawing by Sam Sandoval. (CSKT).

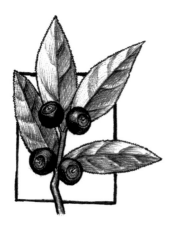

Huckleberry branch.
Drawing by Sam Sandoval. (CSKT).

portant, particularly among the Pend d'Oreille. The *sqélixʷ* knew in great detail the habits and seasonal patterns of fish, and we used this expert knowledge to harvest them whenever needed, using weirs, fish traps, hooks and lines, and gaffing tools. We air-dried fish and stored them for use as winter food. Many places throughout the aboriginal territory were named for the great numbers of fish that could be caught there, including Nʔaycčstm (Place of the Large Bull Trout—the Bonner area), Epɫ X̣ʷy̓ú (Has Whitefish—the outlet of Seeley Lake), and Iɫíx̣ʷ (Something Woven, referring to a fish trap—the Dayton area).

Salish and Pend d'Oreille people also frequently traveled west to get salmon. We would do the fishing ourselves or trade with the tribes of the west, exchanging bitterroot or camas or deer hides or other specialties for salmon.[10] The Salish usually went over the Bitterroot Range to the Salmon, Selway, Lochsa, or Clearwater rivers, while the Pend d'Oreille more often moved down our "road to the West"—the Clark's Fork River—to the drainages below Nčmm̓cí (Lake Pend d'Oreille).

By late summer and early fall, other foods become ripe. In the high country, the people harvested the nuts of the *sčiɫpálqʷ* (whitebark pine), which were high in fats and oils. And in the valleys, the Salish gathered *ċk̓ʷik̓ʷ* (elderberries) and also the bitter white berries of the *stetčcxʷ* (red osier dogwood, also called red willow). Other tribes sometimes called the Salish the "people of the red osier dogwood" because this plant grew so profusely in the Bitterroot Valley.

At the same time, the people gathered *ɫx̣ʷɫó* (choke-cherries), one of our main foods. The pits of chokecherries contain trace amounts of cyanide, which can make animals or people sick if they consume large quantities. When the pits are crushed and exposed to air, however, the cyanide dissipates. And this is exactly what the people have always done. Chokecherries were thoroughly pounded with a stone mortar and pestle. They were often formed into small cakes and then dried and stored. Chokecherry cakes were among the foods that the Salish offered to Lewis and Clark when they arrived in K̓ʷtíɫ P̓upɫm̓ (Ross's Hole) in 1805.

With the fall came more hunting. Aside from the trips east to hunt buffalo, the Salish and Pend d'Oreille relied upon the abundant game resources west of the Continental Divide. Buffalo existed there too, although not in the immense herds that roamed the plains. But Salish territory also teemed with deer and elk, although their numbers fluctuated across the seasons and the land. The elders have told that there were some animals that were put here to be food for the people, and some that were not. Grizzly bears, for example, were not hunted.

The men hunted with bows constructed from the extremely hard wood of the *ckʷn̓čálqʷ* (pacific yew tree), sometimes backed with the boiled horn of bighorn sheep. Whenever the men returned with game, the meat would be divided up equally among all the camps, regardless of which hunters were successful.

There were many favorite hunting areas. One place, near present-day Deer Lodge, was so reliable for hunting *puwé* (mule deer) that it was called Sncwéi̓mn, a

Josephine Camille, Sarah Ogden Magpie, Lucy Camille and baby at the July celebration, Arlee, c. 1910.

Above right: *Fishing at Flathead Lake, c. 1915.*

word that means "place where something is cached." In the ravines near there, the people would construct enclosures of fir branches, drive the deer into them, and often take one hundred deer at a time. But as the elders have told, the hunters would spare whatever deer they did not need. And so our ancestors could return, year after year, to this "cache" of deer.

Fall was also the most common time for burning the undergrowth in the forests. Of all the tools at the disposal of our people, the deliberate and skillful use of fire was perhaps the most powerful way of managing our sprawling territory. Throughout many of the lowland valleys of western Montana, the Salish and Pend d'Oreille set fires when necessary; and over the millennia, this judicious and highly knowledgeable use of fire helped create and maintain an environment that was both pleasant to live in and bountiful in its resources. The Salish set fires often enough to prevent the accumulation of brush, so that the fires usually burned at a low intensity, leaving the older, more fire-resistant trees unharmed. The result was a mix of prairies and open, park-like forests dominated by large, thick-barked trees such as ponderosa pine. Other ecosystems, such as high-altitude forests of *manínⱡp* (subalpine fir), were burned less often. And many other places that were further from centers of population were not intensively managed and were densely wooded and brushy.

The Salish and Pend d'Oreille used fire for many reasons. Used properly, fire helped increase the natural production of berries and other foods and medicines. It helped increase forage for deer, and it stimulated the

growth of grasses for horse herds. It facilitated easier travel. It reduced the danger of larger fires by preventing the buildup of brushy fuel. The open forests of gigantic ponderosas, cottonwoods, and larches imparted a feeling of peace and tranquility to many areas; for the *sqélixʷ*, these great trees gave sustenance both spiritually and materially.

From Lewis and Clark onward, non-Indian visitors to Salish-Pend d'Oreille territory recorded their observations of landscapes that—unbeknownst to them—were the product of our long, careful use of fire. Many journals from the nineteenth century describe the pleasant, open prairies that once characterized the Bitterroot Valley, or the open cathedrals of ancient ponderosa pines and larch that once predominated in sections of the Clark's Fork Valley. Some early visitors did remark upon the frequency and extent of Indian burnings, but few,

Far left: *Čƚeʔews (Three Bellies or Mary Red Crow) pounding chokecherries, c. 1934.*

Above: *Pend d'Oreille family near Snyelʼmn (St. Ignatius), 1906.*

if any, realized that they were witnessing native management of these areas through the use of fire. Spurred by a view of fire as wholly destructive, non-Indians began preventing Salish and Pend d'Oreille people from lighting our usual fires by the mid-nineteenth century. And in the twentieth century, the U.S. Forest Service began suppressing even the occasional lightning-caused fire, while they clear-cut the ancient trees. The result is a transformed landscape; both the old trees and the countless "prairies" described by Lewis and Clark are now gone, for the most part, replaced by thickets, dense forests, and clear-cuts.

As fall turned to winter, the men began trapping fur-bearing animals, such as beaver, which were used for food, medicine and clothing. They moved to winter camps that were selected for shelter from the weather, access to good wood and good fishing, and security from enemies. By the time of the Lewis and Clark expedition, as we have mentioned, most of the Salish were making their winter camps in the Bitterroot Valley.

When the winter cold really set in, the people brought out the Coyote stories, the stories of creation and of how the world came to be. The women would continue to work on hides, making clothing, moccasins, and tipis. The men would repair and construct tools and weapons. Around the new year, the people would conduct jump dances, the prayer dances of thanksgiving for the past year and of hope for the coming year. Through the cold months before the arrival of spring we relied largely on the diverse foods that were dried and stored in the warm months.

Oftentimes, the end of winter was a time of scarcity, and the people looked forward to the appearance of *sⱡťitiči* (pussy willows) and the return of *sx̣ax̣lč* (robins) and *ičⱡá* (blackbirds). They knew spring was coming, and with it the return of the bitterroot.

The yearly cycle of life of the Salish and Pend d'Oreille people was based on a deep spiritual connection to the land, on a finely honed ability to care for and harvest its bounty, and on an intimate knowledge of its fluctuating cycles across seasons and years and even centuries. In this spare portrait, we have made no mention of dozens of other foods that were important to the Salish, nor of the enormous tribal pharmacopoeia—the hundreds of medicinal plants and their uses. But we hope, with this brief introduction, that readers can begin to gain a better sense of our traditional way of life—a way of life that had shaped, for millennia, the land that Lewis and Clark so briefly traversed in 1805 and 1806.

Salish family in the Bitterroot Valley, c. 1885.

A Salish Journey through the Bitterroot Valley

Introduction

In the pages that follow, we will take readers on a tour of selected Salish places and placenames in the Missoula area and the Bitterroot Valley. This cultural geography provides another angle of entry into the traditional Salish-Pend d'Oreille world that Lewis and Clark were entering in 1805. For embedded in these placenames, in the stories of places, in the ways these places were used by tribal people from time immemorial, are further clues to the tribal way of life and the tribal relationship with the land. Countless readers and travelers have set about retracing the route of Lewis and Clark. In the following pages, we offer the opportunity to travel these paths in a different way—in the realization that long before Lewis and Clark, these were Salish and Pend d'Oreille trails. And before that, they were the trails created by Coyote and the animal people at the beginning of time.

This tour of selected Salish placenames in the Bitterroot Valley and adjoining areas offers readers a glimpse of a larger ethnogeographic project that the Salish-Pend d'Oreille Culture Committee has been working on for over a decade. That larger work examines placenames throughout the aboriginal territory and will culminate in the publication of a comprehensive geography of the Salish and Pend d'Oreille people. For that project we have scoured tribal sources, ethnographies, government records, secondary sources, and other materials in an attempt to recover any information relating to the traditional tribal use of the aboriginal territory. We have undertaken extensive trips into the field with tribal elders. We have worked with linguists and tribal experts in the Salish language in an ongoing effort to pin down the precise phonetic composition and meaning of these ancient words.

Linguists say that many of the traditional placenames in the Bitterroot Valley and other areas throughout the vast aboriginal territory are among the oldest words in the Salish language. Some placenames, like Kʷtił Pupłm (Coming Out into a Big Open Place—Ross's Hole), simply describe a place or the foods or other materials that could be found there. As we have already seen, other placenames come from tribal creation stories—the stories of Coyote and the creation of the

The Bitterroot River.

world as we know it. From Tmsmłí (No Salmon—Lolo) to Snetetšé (Place of the Sleeping Baby—Sleeping Child Hot Springs), these are placenames rooted in the stories of how Coyote prepared the world for the human beings who were yet to come and left the signs of his deeds upon the land:

Tlʹ šeẏ u x̣eyƚ x̣ʷeʔúlexʷ	From here there are many places,
ƚu uƚ ʔamtqné,	like ʔamtqné,
uƚ Snq̓ʷeymncú,	and Snq̓ʷeymncú,
uƚ Snk̓ʷƚx̣ʷex̣ʷemi.	and Snk̓ʷƚx̣ʷex̣ʷemi.
L še u x̣ʷʔit sck̓ʷuls ƚu Snčlʹé.	This is where Coyote did many things.
K̓ʷemt t še u šiẏú	Coyote went through there,
nčcnšncu u ċspnuys	going all around and getting rid of
ƚu k̓ʷtk̓ʷtunt x̣ʷix̣ʷeẏúƚ.	all the huge animals.

Pete Beaverhead[1]

In the Coyote stories, we can begin to see how tribal spirituality is deeply tied to the land itself, and how the homeland is filled with spiritual meaning. And while the Bitterroot Valley is a small slice of the overall aboriginal territory of the Salish and Pend d'Oreille, it stands at the heart of both the creation stories and the tribe's history, from the encounter with Lewis and Clark to our long struggle against forced removal to the Flathead Indian Reservation. We will touch more on that history in "Lewis and Clark in the Fold of Tribal History" in Part 2 of this volume. For now, it is enough to say that even today, over a century after our forced removal, the Bitterroot remains a cherished homeland, a place tribal people return to often to pray, to reflect, and to reconnect with our ancestral homeland.

On the following pages, we present a small sampling of the traditional placenames in the Bitterroot Valley and the surrounding area (see map on p. 40). The tour begins just south of the Flathead Reservation boundary, at the base of Evaro Hill. We head south through the Missoula area, with a detour east to a couple of places along the Clark's Fork and Blackfoot rivers. But for the bulk of our tour, we proceed south through the Bitterroot Valley, ending at K̓ʷtíƚ P̓upx̣m (Ross's Hole) and Sk̓ʷumcné Sewƚk̓ʷs (the Big Hole), along the same native trails that Lewis and Clark followed in 1805 and 1806.

We have selected examples of several kinds of place-names—some that originate from the Coyote stories, some in the vicinity of modern-day towns and cities, and some of particular relevance to the Salish encounter with Lewis and Clark.

We hope that readers will understand the leap of faith taken by tribal elders in deciding to share these names with the public. Over time, countless cultural sites in the aboriginal territory have been desecrated, vandalized, and in some cases destroyed by thoughtless people. In sharing even the following limited selection of placenames, the elders are again taking a risk, in the hope that this time their opening up to the world will not lead to further damage to these places, but instead will help nurture understanding and respect for Salish people and Salish culture.

Above left: *Elders on placename research field trip, Blackfoot River valley, 1997.* Left to right: *John Peter Paul, Joe Cullooyah, Agnes Pokerjim Paul, Dolly Linsebigler, Octave Finley.*

Overleaf: *Moon over the Bitterroot Valley.*

Salish-Pend d'Oreille Placenames

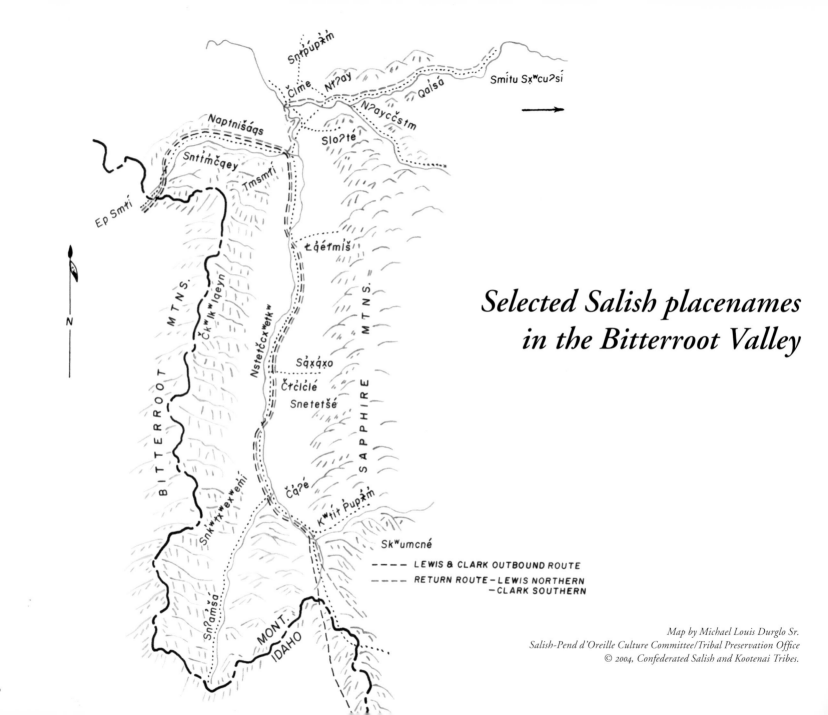

Snɫpupx̣m̓

Smítu Sx̌ʷcuʔsi

Číme Nt̓ʔay Qałsá

NʔayccÉstm

Sloʔté

Naptnišáqs

Snttmčqey

Tmsmɫí

Ep Smɫí

ł̣q̓éɫmiš

Čk̓ʷlk̓ʷlqeyn

Nstełčcx̌ʷetkʷ

Sq̓x̣q̓xo

Čtčíclé

Snetetšé

Čq̓ʔé

Snkʷłx̌ʷex̌ʷemí

Kʷtít Pupx̣m̓

Skʷumcné

Snʔamsa

MONT.
IDAHO

*Selected Salish placenames
in the Bitterroot Valley*

BITTERROOT MTNS.

SAPPHIRE MTNS.

N

- - - - LEWIS & CLARK OUTBOUND ROUTE
— — — RETURN ROUTE – LEWIS NORTHERN
 – CLARK SOUTHERN

*Map by Michael Louis Durglo Sr.
Salish-Pend d'Oreille Culture Committee/Tribal Preservation Office*
© *2004, Confederated Salish and Kootenai Tribes.*

Snⱡpú(pⱡm̓)

Sources for all placenames can be found in the notes section.

Translation: Place Where You Come Out to a Clear Area.

Linguistic analysis: *Sn* = place; *ⱡ* = diminutive or connoting familiarity or affection; *p̓upⱡm̓* = to emerge from a narrow place, as a canyon, into an open flat place. The short form of this placename —*Snⱡpú*—connotes this specific place and what happened in the Coyote story about this place, when some of the animal-people ran out of the monster's anus. The long form—*Snⱡp̓upⱡm̓*—is more of a generic description of this type of landform, when one exits a canyon or forest into a clear open place.

English name or description: The base of Evaro Hill.

About this placename: Like so many other Salish-Pend d'Oreille placenames throughout western Montana, this one comes from the traditional creation stories. Placenames such as Snⱡpú(pⱡm̓) are among the oldest in the language.

In this story, as in many others, Coyote kills one of the *naⱡisqélixʷ*—the people-eaters or monsters—in order to prepare the world for the human beings, to make the world a good place for them. One of the *naⱡisqé* was a great swallowing monster that occupied the Jocko Valley. The place called Snⱡpú was his anus.

There are different versions of this story told by different Salish and Pend d'Oreille elders. What follows is a summary of one version.

Coyote was traveling up the Clark's Fork and Flathead rivers, coming east. Along the way, he mistakenly stepped on Meadowlark's legs. Meadowlark told Coyote that he was going to warn Coyote about something, but since Coyote broke Meadowlark's legs, he wouldn't tell Coyote anything. So Coyote, the first medicine man, apologized to Meadowlark and told him it was an accident, and then he made a splint out of twigs, and wrapped it with sinew, and fixed Meadowlark's legs. So Meadowlark, forgiving Coyote's mistake and grateful for his doctoring, told Coyote that up ahead was a great swallowing monster who devoured everything and everyone. He told Coyote he must go around the monster or die. Coyote thanked Meadowlark and told him his sinew would leave stripes on Meadowlark's leg to show all who came later that he had helped Coyote.

Coyote thought about what Meadowlark told him, and he looked up to the hillside and saw a great *caqʷlš* or western larch. Using his powers, he pulled it out of the ground and threw it over his shoulder. He believed

41

At Snⱡpúpⱡm, October 2003. Left to right: *Josephine Quequesah, Felicite Sapiel McDonald, Michael Louis Durglo Sr., Shirley Trahan, Sadie Peone.*

the huge tree would keep the *naⱡisqé* from being able to swallow him.

Coyote walked along and began noticing that it had become dark, and that there were many dead and dying and starving animal-people along the trail. He asked someone where this monster was. They laughed and told him that he was already inside of it. The monster was so enormous that Coyote and his tree had already been swallowed, and he hadn't even realized it.

High above, the gigantic heart of the monster could be seen, hanging down and beating. Coyote tied his flint knife onto his head and began to jump dance. He rose high, and his flint knife began to cut the monster's heart. Finally he got high enough and climbed onto the monster's heart. He cut off pieces and threw them down to the starving animal-people who were still alive, and the heart meat helped them get stronger. He called out to them, and told them to get ready to run out fast. Some say that at the monster's mouth, in Ravalli Canyon, Coyote placed a great willow hoop to prop the mouth open and allow the animal-people to escape.

Coyote then ran back to the monster's stomach, around the place called Čxʷtpmnwé (Jocko Hollow). There he planted the larch in the ground, saying, "As long as this tree grows, people won't forget what has happened in this place." It was the only larch in that area, and it stood until it was chopped down around the

Salish elder Agnes Pokerjim Paul and daughter Josephine Quequesah at former site of larch planted by Coyote.

anus—Snⱡp̓u. So those animal-people, including Coyote, generally emerged into our world as smaller creatures. As the monster died, he began to convulse, and the anus opened and contracted. That is why some creatures, like ants, are pinched around their middles. Bed Bug and Tick were the last ones out of the monster's anus, and so they were flattened.

Pend d'Oreille elders used to tease Salish elders, saying that they came out the monster's rear end, since their homeland was to the south, while the Pend d'Oreille, who lived to the north, emerged from the mouth.

Elders have told how Snⱡp̓ú(pⱡm̓) has always been an important camping area for the people. Many remembered camping there and grazing their horses on the surrounding hills. They did this well into the twentieth century, when non-Indian development and the establishment of private property forced them to quit.

Elders and anthropologists have both told of the trails leading through Snⱡp̓ú(pⱡm̓)—heading north toward the Jocko and Mission valleys, heading south across the Clark's Fork River near Q̓ʷɂeⱡ (Frenchtown) to the hunting area around ɂamtqné, and heading southeast toward Nⱡɂay (Missoula). Those people who were traveling up the Clark's Fork River would often take a trail east from Snⱡp̓ú(pⱡm̓) around the back side of Nm̓q̓ʷé (Mt. Jumbo) in order to avoid being ambushed in Hellgate Canyon. So Snⱡp̓ú(pⱡm̓) was a place that connected the Missoula area, Clark's Fork River valley, and Bitterroot Valley with the Jocko and Flathead rivers to the north.

time of World War I. Elders have told that it stood up for two days after it was sawed completely through.

Then Coyote took his flint knife and cut the monster's heart off. Some storytellers say it formed a hill near the old Jocko Agency. Others say it formed the heart-shaped bare spot high on the mountain ridge on the east side of the Jocko Valley.

The monster began to collapse and die. It is said that those animals that are large in size in our world today—elk, buffalo, bear, moose, and many others—ran out through the mouth. Other creatures were not so fast, or were situated in a different part of the monster's insides. They had to run over Evaro hill, and out the monster's

Člmé

Translation: Tree Limb Cut Off.

Linguistic analysis: *Člmé* means one limb or branch has been cut off. *Člmlmé* means more than one has been cut off. *Ta eps čsčstté* means it has no limbs.

English name or description: A major camp in Grass Valley, around the area known as Council Grove, just west of Missoula.

About this placename: This placename refers to a traditional Salish-Pend d'Oreille camp along the north side of the Clark's Fork River, which in July 1855 served as the site of negotiations between tribal leaders and U.S. government officials. Those negotiations concluded with the signing of the Hellgate Treaty, which established the Jocko or Flathead Indian Reservation.

Člmé is an area rich in chokecherries, an important food harvested in September. Elders have told of rare white chokecherries that grew there. Salish and Pend d'Oreille people knew this area as a good winter grazing place for our horses.

Člmé is also near one of the important fords of the Clark's Fork River, a place called Ncx̣ʷoteẁs (Something Growing by the Edge of the Water). From this place, major trails lead in all directions. To the north, the trails led through Snɫp̓ú(p̓x̓m̓), up Evaro Hill, and into the Jocko and Mission valleys. To the south, trails led toward Tmsmɫí (Lolo) and the Bitterroot Valley, and over the mountains into Idaho. To the west, people continued by foot, horseback, and canoe down the Clark's Fork River toward Q̓ʷʔeɫ (Frenchtown) and all the way into what is now northern Idaho and Washington state. And to the east lay Nɫʔay (Missoula) and the trail up the Clark's Fork and Blackfoot rivers, the main routes taken to buffalo, east of the mountains.

Člmé assumed special importance in tribal history with the signing of the Hellgate Treaty. As we describe in the concluding segment of this book, the treaty was a defining moment in the recent history of the Salish, Pend d'Oreille, and Kootenai people, and it continues to form the legal framework for the relationship between the United States government and the Confederated Salish and Kootenai Tribes.

The area near Člmé also became the site of the first non-Indian settlements in the Missoula Valley, with the establishment of Frank Worden and C. P. Higgins's store in 1863.

But long before the 1855 treaty, and in the years since, Člmé has been a place of great importance to the Salish and Pend d'Oreille people.

*Gustavus Sohon's drawing of treaty
negotiations at Člmé (Council Grove),
July 1855.*

Nⱡʔay(cčstm)

Translation: Place of the Small Bull Trout. Alternatively spelled Nⱡćay(cčstm).

Linguistic analysis: N = place or locative; ⱡʔay = small or immature bull trout. ʔay (alternately spelled c̓i by some linguists) is the word for large, very mature bull trout—as elder John Peter Paul said, "the really big ones." Łʔay (alternately spelled ⱡc̓i by linguists) is the word for younger, "regular-sized" (or immature) bull trout.

English name or description: Missoula; specifically, the confluence of Rattlesnake Creek and the Clark's Fork River.

About this placename: Nⱡʔaycčstm, or Nⱡʔay, refers to the whole Missoula area, although it originally referred to a major camp where Rattlesnake Creek flows into the Clark's Fork River, just across the river from the University of Montana. As the name implies, this was an important and abundant place for catching bull trout—usually the smaller, younger ones. The people traditionally fished with hook and line and with a variety of fish traps. The fish would be cooked and eaten right away or dried and stored for eating in winter. Louie Adams (b. 1933) tells that his maternal grandmother, Louise, was born at Nⱡʔay, next to the Clark's Fork River where the University of Montana is now located. Her mother was camped there while her father, Victor Vanderburg (1868–1939), fished for bull trout.

Nⱡʔay was probably even more important as a place for gathering another staple: sṗeⱡm (bitterroot). As Salish elder Eneas Pierre (1905–1985) told us, bitterroot in some parts of the Bitterroot Valley were too bitter, because at the beginning, Coyote burned them. But the sqélixʷ and members of other tribes always went to Nⱡʔay, where the bitterroot were plentiful, easy to dig, and good tasting.

Every spring, the people would camp for several weeks in many locations around the Missoula area—including such places as the entrance to Hellgate Canyon and the base of Mount Jumbo (called Nmq̓ʷé); the area around what is now the Missoula fairgrounds (called Snačⱡq̇eẏmín—Place of the School—because of the nearby University of Montana); the South Hills area near Miller Creek; and a large section on the west side of Missoula, including Fort Missoula, the Reserve Street area, and sites along the Clark's Fork and Bitterroot rivers.

For many decades, the city of Missoula coexisted with the ancient seasonal cycle of the sqélixʷ. The people often camped in the area around Reserve Street, before it was covered over by Shopko and its parking lot. They hauled water from the nearby wells of accommo-

dating *suyapis* (non-Indians), and dug for bitterroot in the surrounding open fields, including near Fort Missoula. Tribal people sometimes rode streetcars between their camps and the digging grounds. Salish elder Mary Kizer (1880–1965) used to take the bus from Arlee to the area near the intersection of Highway 93 and Interstate 90, before there was an interstate. She would dig bitterroot all day, and then take the bus home. Many of the current Salish and Pend d'Oreille elders profiled at the end of this book—people generally born between 1910 and 1940—have memories of camping in undeveloped areas around Missoula while their families dug bitterroot. Today, elders still remember the camps used by many families—the Sapiels, the Vanderburgs, the Adamses, the Cullooyahs, the Lumprys, the Lamooses, the Antoines, the Pauls, the Pokerjims, the Ninepipes, the Combses, and many others.

For many years, then, Salish and Pend d'Oreille people continued to utilize the Missoula area in the traditional way, even as the city slowly grew. But this cultural coexistence became increasingly difficult in the second half of the twentieth century, as developers paved over many of the cherished bitterroot places. Nmq̓ʷé is now partly buried beneath Interstate 90, the Eastgate Shopping Mall, and other roads and buildings. The Missoula fairgounds area was used by people until the 1910s or 1920s, when houses and streets expanded into that district. Tribal people continued to utilize the west side of Missoula from what is now the headquarters of the Montana Power Company south to the Highway 93 strip until the 1950s and 1960s, when development began to spread into those areas as well. With the recent massive expansion of commercial development along Reserve Street, the old landscape of the *sqélixʷ* along the west side of Missoula—a bountiful land that had supplied the people with food since the dawn of human history in the area—was practically wiped out.

Although Missoula was one of the most important bitterroot grounds, the *sqélixʷ* also used many other places throughout the aboriginal territory, including Camas Prairie, the Flathead River corridor, the West Fork of the Bitterroot, the Helena area, the Anaconda

Nⱡʔay—Rattlesnake Creek and Clark's Fork River, Missoula, MT. *Oil painting by Tony Sandoval, 2003.*

area, and the Big Hole Valley. In some places, including in the Anaconda area and also a place called Ep Sṗeⱡm (Has Bitterroot) high up the West Fork of the Bitterroot River, bitterroots could be dug as late as July. To this day, many of these places continue to be utilized by the people for harvesting *sṗeⱡm*.

Sloʔté

Translation: Two Valleys Coming Together to Make One Little Valley.

Linguistic analysis: May contain the root *loót* (alternate spelling: *lčʷót*), meaning valley.

English name or description: Pattee Canyon, on the southeast side of Missoula, and the route of a trail that leads over a saddle to Deer Creek and down to an important ford of the Clark's Fork River across from Nʔaycčstm (the confluence of the Clark's Fork and Blackfoot rivers at Bonner).

About this placename: Just as *Nɫʔay* is strongly associated with the seasonal activities of springtime—gathering bitterroot and fishing for bull trout—so *Sloʔté* is linked to another aspect of the traditional cycle of life—going east to hunt buffalo.

Over the millennia, the Salish and Pend d'Oreille developed a wide-ranging, complex trail system throughout their vast territories, and several routes connected the lands west of the mountains with the buffalo grounds to the east. Salish and Pend d'Oreille people would often travel up the Clark's Fork River on their way to the prairies east of the Continental Divide.

For those traveling from the Bitterroot Valley, it was sometimes desirable to avoid Hellgate Canyon, where in later years Blackfeet raiders would try to ambush smaller parties. The canyon could also be an especially narrow passage when water ran high in the Clark's Fork River in late spring and early summer. For these reasons, Sloʔté was an important route. Parties going east from the Bitterroot Valley could ride up Pattee Canyon, over a small pass, and then down Deer Creek, which leads to an easy ford of the Clark's Fork, just across from Nʔaycčstm (Bonner). From there, travelers could continue up the Clark's Fork River or the Blackfoot River, which enters the Clark's Fork at Nʔaycčstm. If they went up the Clark's Fork, they would continue to Snx̣ʷq̓ʷpuʔsaqs (Junction of Two Trails, now called Garrison Junction), then over McDonald Pass to Čɫmlšé (Helena), and on to the Musselshell River, or south to the Yellowstone country. If they went up the Blackfoot River, they would climb over Łatatí Sx̣ʷcuʔsí (Cadotte's Pass) or Smítu Sx̣ʷcuʔsí (Lewis and Clark Pass) to the Dearborn River, the Sun River, and the Missouri River country, and then on to the Sweetgrass Hills.

Sometimes the Salish traveled east from the Hamilton area over the more rugged Skalkaho Pass (see the entry for Sq̓x̣q̓x̣ó). At other times, they went over through the Big Hole Valley and from there to the Yellowstone area, Three Forks, the Missouri River, or the Musselshell River.

Left: *Salish elder Eneas Vanderburg at Sloʔté, October 2003.*

Below: *Looking down Deer Creek toward Nʔaycčstm (Bonner).*

Top Right: *Nʔaycčstm, Sept. 1997. Cultural leader Johnny Arlee (far left, in blue jacket) and Salish-Pend d'Oreille elders and students.*

Bottom right: *Salish elder Eneas Vanderburg reviewing cultural information on the area.*

In more recent years, the area around Sloʔté continued to serve as an important camp for people digging bitterroot in the Missoula area. During the bitterroot season, people regularly conducted horse races in the Sloʔté area.

Nʔaycčstm

Translation: Place of the Big Bull Trout. Alternatively spelled Nˢicčstm.

Linguistic analysis: N = place; ʔaycčstm = large bull trout. John Peter Paul noted that ʔay is the word for large, mature bull trout. Łʔay is the word for younger, smaller bull trout.

English name or description: Confluence of the Big Blackfoot and Clark's Fork rivers at Bonner, Montana.

About this placename: As noted in the entry for Sloʔté, Nʔaycčstm was a major junction in the trail system of the Salish and Pend d'Oreille, connecting the Clark's Fork and Blackfoot rivers. The route up the Blackfoot led east over Smítu Sx̣ʷcuʔsí (Lewis and Clark Pass) and Łatatí Sx̣ʷcuʔsí (Cadotte's Pass) to the Dearborn River, the Sun River, the Missouri River, and beyond to the Sweetgrass Hills. Travelers could also turn north at the junction with the Clearwater River and go toward Seeley Lake and on to the Swan Valley.

Just as Nłʔay was named for immature bull trout and was an important fishing place, so Nʔaycčstm was named for the mature bull trout and was a key place for harvesting these large fish. Agnes Pokerjim Paul (b. 1910) remembers camping along the river during fall hunting trips just upstream from Bonner. The men would fish along the Clark's Fork just upstream from Nʔaycčstm.

Qaˈsá or Epɫ ítx̣ʷeʔ

Translation: *Qaˈsá* apparently refers to wet ground where camas is plentiful; *Epɫ ítx̣ʷeʔ* means "It Has Camas."

Linguistic analysis: The ethnographer James Teit reported that *Skalsá* came from a word possibly referring to camas in the language of the Smtiʔus, an extinct Salishan tribe whose headquarters were situated in the Potomac area. Teit said the Salish and Pend d'Oreille also referred to this area as Epɫéthwa (in current spelling, Epɫ ítx̣ʷeʔ). *Ítx̣ʷeʔ* refers to baked camas; *sx̣ʷeʔli* refers to raw camas. Elders today report having heard both *Qaˈsá* and *Epɫ ítx̣ʷeʔ* as placenames referring to this area.

English name or description: Camas digging grounds near Potomac, Montana, along Union Creek and Camas Creek, tributaries of the Blackfoot.

About this placename: Qaˈsá, or Epɫ ítx̣ʷeʔ, was perhaps the most important camas digging ground in all of western Montana. The broad, open valley, maintained by tribal people with the careful application of periodic fire, was a great sea of camas, and many western tribes would journey there to partake of the abundance. Salish, Upper and Lower Pend d'Oreille or Kalispel, Spokane, Coeur d'Alene, Nez Perce, Kootenai, and many others came to Qaˈsá, or Epɫ ítx̣ʷeʔ, often on their way

to buffalo in early summer. Qaˈsá, or Epɫ ítx̣ʷeʔ, was also important as a hunting area in the fall.

Top: *Agnes Pokerjim Paul telling Johnny Arlee and others about Sčilíp Qaˈsá—traditional camps near the confluence of the Blackfoot River and Camas Creek, a stream issuing from Qaˈsá or Epɫ ítx̣ʷeʔ. September 1997.*

Bottom: *Cultural student James Bigcrane looks south over Qaˈsá, or Epɫ ítx̣ʷeʔ, September 1997.*

Right: Qaˈsá—Potomac, MT. *Čpaaqn (Morrison Mountain) in background. Oil painting by Tony Sandoval, 2003.*

Smı́tu Sx̣ʷcuʔsı́

Translation: Indian Fort Pass.

Linguistic analysis: *Smı́tu* = word for rock structure for hiding to ambush the enemy; *sx̣ʷcuʔsı́* = pass.

English name or description: Lewis and Clark Pass.

About this placename: In traveling between their western territories and the buffalo plains east of the mountains, Salish and Pend d'Oreille people utilized a sprawling network of trails and an intimate knowledge of the most accessible passes. Early non-Indian travelers, including Lewis and Clark, also utilized these preexisting routes and passes. Primary Salish-Pend d'Oreille trails led up all the major drainages of western Montana, including the Clark's Fork River, the Little Blackfoot River, and the Blackfoot River. Two major passes crossed the Continental Divide at the head of the Blackfoot River: Smı́tu Sx̣ʷcuʔsı́ (Lewis and Clark Pass) and Łatatı́ Sx̣ʷcuʔsı́ (Cadotte Pass). Travois tracks are still visible in places along some of these trails.

Other tribes also traveled on these trails. Tribes from the west used them to go to buffalo; the Nez Perce name for the trail leading up the Blackfoot River and over Smı́tu Sx̣ʷcuʔsı́ is k'uysey'ne'iskit, meaning bison hunt trail. The Blackfeet also used these trails to venture into Salish-Pend d'Oreille territory on raids. For this reason, Salish and Pend d'Oreille warriors constructed small

stone "forts," called *smı́tu*, on some passes in order to watch for approaching enemy parties. That is why this pass is called Smı́tu Sx̣ʷcuʔsı́.

Elders and Tribal Preservation staff at Smı́tu Sx̣ʷcuʔsı́, May 2003. Noel Pichette, Tim Ryan, Eneas Vanderburg, Wes Benn.

Tmsmɫi

Translation: No Salmon.

Linguistic analysis: *Tm* = contraction of tam, meaning no, none; *smɫi* = salmon.

English name or description: Lolo; the area where Lolo Creek empties into the Bitterroot River.

About this placename: Although most Montana history books trace the history of the Lolo area to the Lewis and Clark expedition and their christening of it as "Travelers' Rest," the older tribal relationship with this place, ironically, was reflected in Meriwether Lewis's journals. Lewis reported seeing, along Lolo Creek, "many of the pine trees peeled off"—ponderosa pines that had been stripped of bark by the Salish to procure the sweet inner cambium layer of the bark for food. Several members of the expedition also remarked on other signs of tribal use of the area, and described at length the particularly profuse and varied bird life and flora around Lolo.

Tmsmɫi was always an area of special importance to the Salish and Pend d'Oreille because of those abundant resources. It was a favorite hunting area, especially for deer, and the people would move there for that purpose in the spring. The expedition members reported, on their return to Traveler's Rest in July 1806, that their hunters were able to bring in "many deer," and "the Indians" told them that "great numbers" of mountain goats could be found in the Bitterroot Mountains.

We also knew Tmsmɫi as a place where a great variety of edible and medicinal plants grew in profusion, and Lewis also noted this in his journals. That bounty was in part the product of the systematic and careful tribal use of fire over countless years.

But like many other Salish-Pend d'Oreille placenames, *Tmsmɫi* also reflects a tribal relationship with this place extending back even further—to the time before human beings. Like Snɫpu(pàm̓), Tmsmɫi is one of the placenames that originates in the Coyote stories. Tmsmɫi (No Salmon) takes its name from the story of Coyote trying, but failing, to bring salmon over the Bitterroot Mountains into what is now western Montana. As in the stories about Snɫpú, there are some minor variations in the stories told by the elders about Tmsmɫi. What follows is a summary of some versions of that story.

As Coyote set out on his eastward journey, he said that the salmon would follow him upstream—even up the little streams, wherever he turned off to visit the various animal and bird nations. If he were welcomed, the salmon would always go there; but if he were not welcomed, he would create a waterfall to block their passage. This is how it went during Coyote's journeys in the area now known as Washington State.

Coyote's route eventually took him into what would become Salish and Pend d'Oreille territory—through the Jocko Valley, across the Missoula area, up the Bitterroot Valley, and then up Lolo Creek, where he stayed quite a while resting. While resting, he thought about his earlier travels on the west side of the mountains and how the salmon followed him up the streams. He decided he wanted to do something to bring the salmon to the east side of the mountains, into the Bitterroot drainage.

So Coyote went over to Epsmłí (It Has Salmon), the Lochsa and Clearwater rivers, where he planned to get a salmon and carry it over the mountains. He said he wanted do this so "there will be food for the people in this part of the country." He managed to catch a big salmon. A voice told him that he could indeed take the fish over the Bitterroot Range, but if he failed, there would be no way to change it. The voice told him he must cover the salmon in fresh, green grass, and then carry it over the range, and be sure not to stop until he got across the pass. The voice repeated this warning not to stop.

So Coyote started carrying Salmon up the mountains. But Salmon wanted to remain in his home country, so he used his *sumeš*, his power, to make the pack get heavier. Coyote got tired and very thirsty. He saw the tops of the mountains not far ahead. Near the top of the range, Coyote found Salmon just too heavy to carry. He figured it wouldn't hurt to rest, so he sat down. Some say Coyote—being Coyote—stopped on the pass to urinate or defecate. Salmon used the opportunity to

slide out of the pack, and because he was so slippery, he got away. Where Salmon hit the ground, he made a bubbling spring burst forth from the ground, and the water carried the fish back to Epsmłí.

Coyote said that from that time on, Lolo Creek, on the east side of the Bitterroot Range, would be called Tmsmłí (No Salmon). He said that people would make a trail over the mountains to get their salmon to the west. To make up for his failure, Coyote said he would

Tmsmłí—Lolo, MT. *Oil painting by Tony Sandoval, 2003.*

make other foods for tribes to the east of Lolo Pass. And Coyote also made a warm spring come forth, where people could come in the springtime to heal themselves. In Salish this place is called Sntȋm̓čqey (see the entry for this placename); in English it is called Lolo Hot Springs.

Naptnišá

Translation: Trail to the Nez Perce.

Linguistic analysis: *N* = locative, place; *aptniš* = from *saʔaptní*, Nez Perce people; *á* = trail, from lexical suffix *aqs*.

English name or description: The Lolo Trail.

About this placename: *Naptnišá* is another placename that has its roots in the tribal creation stories. As described in the entry for Tmsmłí, this trail was first prepared by Coyote during his travels.

For millennia, the trail west from Tmsmłí was a link between the Salish and Pend d'Oreille and their friends and allies the Nez Perce. That is why the Salish called the trail Naptnišá, meaning "trail to the Nez Perce." The Nez Perce called the trail *kʼuyseyʼneʼiskit*, meaning bison hunt trail, for they used it to travel over the mountains, past Lolo, past the Missoula area, and either up the Blackfoot River or up the Clark's Fork River toward the buffalo country. Lewis and Clark recorded this word as best they could, spelling it "Cokahlarishkit." The two tribes traded and intermarried often, especially after the introduction of horses, and to this day many families among the Salish and Pend d'Oreille have Nez Perce blood, and many among the Nez Perce are part Salish or Pend d'Oreille. The old people said the trail continued beyond the Nez Perce country, all the way to the ocean.

Although Salish people used this trail regularly, the expedition members, guided by an elderly Shoshone unfamiliar with the area, found it a difficult route to follow. By contrast, Olin Wheeler, a non-Indian researcher who conducted fieldwork on the Lolo Trail in 1902, found that the trail was still distinct. Wheeler wrote, "a great trail like the Lolo is much like a great trunk line of railway. Here and there, at certain favorable places, will be found lines of parallel trails, like parallel railway sidings, all merging, at some point, onto the main track or trail; branch trails also, like branch lines, will now and again be found. So it was and is here. There are many parallel trails, some of them now dim and overgrown through age and disuse, and there are evidently two or three points where the divide itself may be crossed. The conditions of travel are the same whichever route one takes, and all the trails terminate at the same point, the beautiful summit prairie, or the glades of Glade Creek, down which the party proceeded two miles and camped." Wheeler camped there amid wild strawberries and found numerous old trails "on each side of the valley all converging on our camp."

A number of other important Salish trails link Naptnišá to other areas. One leads north, up Grave Creek, a tributary of Lolo Creek, and over to Ep Snčemčm (It Has Tree Sap, called Petty Creek in English). From there, routes lead on to the Clark's Fork River and other places. Today, a U.S. Forest Service road follows this route. The trail is being restored in a joint effort of the Salish and Nez Perce tribes and the Forest Service.

Felicite Sapiel McDonald along Naptnišá in 2001, describing Salish use of the area. Stephen Smallsalmon and Sophie Haynes listen.

Snt́t́ḿčqey

Translation: Steam on a Ridge Top.

Linguistic analysis: *Sn* = place; *t́iḿ* = damp (probably from the hot springs); *čqey* = ridge top.

English name or description: The area near Lolo Hot Springs.

About this placename: As noted in the Coyote story relating to Tmsmłí, this is a site that also has its origins in the creation stories. After Coyote failed to bring salmon into western Montana, he atoned for his mistake by making a warm spring emerge at Snt́t́ḿčqey, and said this would be a place where people could come to heal themselves. Salish and Pend d'Oreille people soaked often in the hot springs. The regular tribal use of this important healing place was noted in the journals of the Lewis and Clark expedition: "the Indians have formed into a bath [the main hot spring] by stopping the run with stone and pebbles." Near the springs were numerous traditional camp places and camas digging grounds.

Left: *Salish leader Sam Resurrection at Snt́t́ḿčqey, c. 1915.*

Below: *Elders and staff of the Salish-Pend d'Oreille Culture Committee near Snt́t́ḿčqey, 2001.*

Ep Smłí

Translation: It Has Salmon.

Linguistic analysis: *Ep* = It has; *smłí* = salmon.

English name or description: The Lochsa and Clearwater River system.

About this placename: The origins of this placename lie in the same Coyote story that also explains the name for the Lolo area, Tmsmłí (No Salmon); Snt̓m̓čqey (Lolo Hot Springs); and Naptnišá, the trail connecting Tmsmłí and Ep Smłí.

Salish and Pend d'Oreille people often traveled west to get salmon, either by fishing for them (Lewis and Clark noted weirs in the upper reaches of the Lochsa) or by trading with the Nez Perce or other tribes west of the Bitterroot Mountains. Besides the Lolo Trail, Salish people also frequently traveled over many other passes, including those known in English as Lost Trail Pass (into the Salmon River country) and Nez Perce Pass (into the Selway River drainage). The Pend d'Oreille more frequently traveled down the Clark's Fork River—by foot, by canoe, and later by horse—past Sx̌ʷéʔwi (Albeni Falls), on down to the Pend d'Oreille River country in what is now eastern Washington.

Gathering traditional foods and medicines atop Lolo Pass, 2001–2.

Top: *Joe Vanderburg and Tony Incashola looking for x̣asx̣s.*

Left: *Felicite Sapiel McDonald with camas.*

Above: *Galen Hawk with camas.*

Nstetčcxʷetkʷ

Translation: Waters of the Red Osier Dogwood.

Linguistic analysis: *N* = locative prefix indicating place; *stetčcxʷ* = red osier dogwood; *-etkʷ* = suffix indicating water.

English name or description: The Bitterroot River.

About this placename: The Bitterroot River runs through the heart of Salish territory and is lined with camps and other places known to us by their traditional placenames. Salish trails followed both sides of the river from Nⱡʔay (Missoula) all the way past Kʷtiⱡ Pupⱥm (Ross's Hole). Although some sources list Nstetčcxʷetkʷ as the Salish name for the Bitterroot River as a whole, it was probably the name of a particular place along the Bitterroot River where *stetčcxʷ* (red osier dogwood) was the predominant vegetation. (Some tribes called the Salish "the people of the red osier dogwood" in their languages.) In Salish ethnogeography, it is typical to have placenames for numerous points along major rivers, but not for large rivers in their entirety. For example, there are dozens of Salish-Pend d'Oreille placenames for specific places along the Flathead River, which runs through the very center of the Flathead Reservation. But the only name for the river itself is Ntxʷétkʷ, which is the generic word for a large river. Similarly, some tribal elders have said that they never heard the old people say a Salish name for the Bitterroot River or the Bitterroot Valley as a whole. When they were traveling that way, they would just say they were going to Łq̓eⱡmⱡš (Stevensville), Tmsmⱡí (Lolo), Snk̓ʷⱡxʷexʷem̓í (Darby), or other places.

Far right: The Bitterroot River.

Łq̓éⱡmlš

Translation: Wide Cottonwoods.

Linguistic analysis: *Łq̓* = from *ⱡaq̓*, wide or broad; *mlš* from *mulš*, cottonwood.

English name or description: The Stevensville area.

About this placename: Some elders say Łq̓éⱡmlš refers to the particularly wide leaves of the cottonwood trees that grew in the area. Others say the placename refers to the wide girth of the cottonwoods at this place.

Łq̓éⱡmlš was the most important winter camp of the Salish west of the Continental Divide. It was the center of Salish life until the tribe was forced to move north to the Flathead Reservation in 1891 (see "Lewis and Clark in the Fold of Tribal History" in part 2 of this volume). During the winter, the people particularly liked to camp along the east side of the river all the way from Łq̓éⱡmlš (Stevensville) to Čⱡčlčlé (Hamilton), where there was abundant wood, excellent grazing for horses, and good fishing throughout the cold months. In the summer months, berries and camas could be found in abundance nearby. Due to the abundance of bitterroot in the area, early Canadian trappers referred to the area as *racine amere* (the French Canadian term for bitterroot).

Because of the importance of Łq̓éⱡmlš to the Salish, it was here that Jesuit missionaries, led by Pierre Jean de Smet, decided to locate their mission in 1841. The Salish forced the Jesuits to leave in 1849, but the mission was reestablished in the 1860s.

The importance of the area to the Salish was reflected in the Hellgate Treaty negotiations in 1855, when Chief Victor steadfastly refused the U.S. government's demand that the Salish leave the valley. In 1872, when the majority of the Salish again refused to leave the area and move to the Jocko (Flathead) Reservation, they were forced to select individual allotments of land in the Bitterroot Valley. Most Salish chose sites in the vicinity of Łq̓éⱡmlš. Many Salish people also selected or were assigned allotments along nearby Burnt Fork, a tributary of the Bitterroot River.

Top Right: Eneas "Tom Puss" Pierre as baby with his mother, Ann Calasco.

Far right: Salish people at St. Mary's Mission during a return visit to Łq̓éⱡmlš, 1911.

Overleaf: Łq̓éⱡmlš—Stevensville, MT. Oil painting by Tony Sandoval, 2003.

Čkʷlkʷlqéyn

Čkʷlkʷlqey (St. Mary's Peak and Bitterroot Mountains) from St. Mary's Mission, Łq̓eⱡml̓š (Stevensville), December 2000.

Translation: Red-Topped Peaks.

Linguistic analysis: *Č* = on; *kʷlkʷl* = reduplication of *kʷil* (red); *qéyn* = head or peak.

English name or description: Some say this word refers specifically to St. Mary's Peak; others use it to refer to the Bitterroot Range as a whole.

About this placename: This placename derives from the beautiful red color that washes across Čkʷlkʷlqéy(n) when the peaks are struck by the early morning light. Čkʷlkʷlqéy(n) is another placename tied to the time of the Ice Age and the great floods. The elders have told how, in the beginning, the land was covered by water, but high up on Čkʷlkʷlqéy(n), some of the animal-people survived.

The Salish hunted, fished, picked berries, and traveled through the entire length of the Bitterroot Range, and many places in the mountains were and are held sacred by the people.

Čⱡčlčlé

Translation: Elders have offered two translations for this placename: Scattered Trees Growing on Open Ground or Trees Standing in Water.

Linguistic analysis: *Čⱡčlčlé* lends itself to both translations offered by the elders. *Čⱡ* can refer to a clear area or open ground or something flat and smooth (such as a water surface), and *člčlé* can refer either to a bunch of trees or to trees spaced apart from each other (*es člčíl*), growing in a widely spaced or scattered way, without brushy growth between them. Other elders think *Čⱡčlčlé* refers to cottonwood trees that were scattered on the open ground, not close to the river where they usually grow.

English name or description: The Hamilton area.

About this placename: Long before Montana copper baron Marcus Daly established the town of Hamilton in about 1890—indeed, long before members of the Lewis and Clark expedition passed the area on their way to Tmsmⱡí (Lolo) in 1805—Čⱡčlčlé was an important camp for the Salish. It is about midway between Łq̓éⱡml̓š (Stevensville) and Snk̓ʷⱡx̣ʷex̣ʷemí (Darby).

Even in later years, after the Salish had been forced north to the Flathead Reservation, Čⱡčlčlé remained important. In the early twentieth century, as non-Indians developed horticultural farms in the Bitterroot Valley, many Salish and Pend d'Oreille people began to come down to pick fruit—and to visit their cherished homeland. At Čⱡčlčlé, many farms specialized in strawberries. Łq̓éⱡml̓š was known for potatoes. Many Salish people continued to work seasonally in the Bitterroot Valley until mechanization and migrant labor displaced them in the 1950s, and then residential development displaced the farms themselves. Until the late nineteenth century, the Salish enjoyed a life of relative abundance in the Bitterroot Valley. By comparison, the twentieth century was a time of poverty. Most people were truly struggling to get by. Yet the elders today remember the people nevertheless enjoying themselves in the family fruit-picking camps in the Bitterroot Valley.

The translation of *Čⱡčlčlé* as "trees standing in water" refers to a pond, located on the northeast side of Hamilton, in which dead cottonwoods had been standing for as long as anyone could remember.

The translation of *Čⱡčlčlé* as "scattered trees growing on open ground," on the other hand, refers back to the fire-shaped landscape created and maintained by the Salish throughout much of the Bitterroot Valley. Elders such as Andrew Ninepipe used to tell of how, in the Hamilton area, the valley once had very few trees— just a little bunch here or there, separated by open grasslands. When people traveled across those broad prai-

Right: *Salish camp near Čⱡčlčlé, c. 1930.*

Far right: *Looking toward the pass at Sq̓x̣q̓x̣ó.*

66

ries during the hot summer, a mirage would form, and a bunch of trees would appear to be standing in a pool of water. Many of the earliest non-Indian visitors to the Bitterroot Valley, including Lewis and Clark, described many areas as open prairies with only isolated scatterings of trees. After non-Indians took control of the Bitterroot Valley and forced out the Salish people and our practice of regular burnings, those prairies soon filled with brush and trees. In short, one of the translations of *Čłčlčlé*, scattered trees growing on open ground, reflects a vanished cultural landscape.

Sq̓x̣q̓x̣ó

Translation: Many Trails.

Linguistic analysis: *Es q̓ax̣* means trail, road, or tracks. *Sq̓x̣q̓x̣ó* is a plural form. The long form is likely *Sq̓x̣q̓x̣ólex̌*ʷ; the suffix *lex*ʷ refers to land. This placename has sometimes been translated as originating from the term for beaver, *sqlew̓* (plural: *sqlqlew̓*).

English name or description: Skalkaho Pass and the trails leading to it from the Bitterroot Valley.

About this placename: Sq̓x̣q̓x̣ó was one of the passes used by the Salish in moving east from the Bitterroot Valley (see also Sloʔté and Smítu Sx̌ʷcuʔsí). It was known as the steepest of all the routes, and so was used less often when the people moved over the mountains to hunt buffalo. But Sq̓x̣q̓x̣ó was also more direct, leading to the high valleys of upper Rock Creek and on toward Momoo (Anaconda), Snt̓apqey (Butte), and places east and south. Until the mid-nineteenth century, considerable numbers of buffalo could still be found west of the mountains—including in the Flint Creek valley, which could be accessed from the Bitterroot Valley by climbing through Sq̓x̣q̓x̣ó.

At Sq̓x̣q̓x̣ó, October 2003: Sadie Peone, Shirley Trahan, Michael Louis Durglo Sr., Felicite Sapiel McDonald, Josephine Quequesah.

Snetetšé

Translation: Place of the Sleeping Baby.

Linguistic analysis: *Sn* = place; *etetšé* from *es itši*, sleeping.

English name or description: Sleeping Child Hot Springs.

About this placename: Snetetšé is another site from the creation stories—and as such, another placename whose origins predate human history in the region. There are minor variations in the versions told by different elders. What follows is one version.

As Coyote traveled by this place, he heard the sound of a crying baby.

Coyote looked and found a baby at the foot of a little cliff, and tried to comfort it. He looked for its mother, but couldn't find her. He sang lullabies, but that didn't work. He then gave the baby his finger to suck on, and the baby quieted. Coyote fell asleep.

The "baby" kept on sucking, and finally sucked all the flesh off Coyote's bones.

Many days later, Fox came along and saw Coyote's bones. Fox put the bones in a neat pile, and jumped over them.

Coyote came back to life. As always, he thought he was just sleeping.

Fox told him he was dead and that the baby had killed him, because it was really an evil monster. Fox said the baby was one of four monsters in the area. Fox warned Coyote, saying he'd better leave. Then Fox left.

Coyote watched Fox go away. Then he thought about it, and decided he must kill these monsters rather than run away.

He circled back and headed up the trail, pretending to be another traveler. He heard the baby crying again, and he stopped and tied his magic flint knife onto his finger.

He got to the baby and did the same thing as before, pacifying the baby with his finger. As the baby sucked on his finger, Coyote pushed it farther down the baby's throat until he reached its lungs, and then sharply turned his finger and pulled it out, cutting the lungs up.

The baby tore loose of the cradleboard, jumped up, staggered around, and died.

Coyote did not want to kill each of the other three monsters separately, so he schemed to get them to come to a feast. He noticed that game seemed to be scarce around the area.

He dug a deep hole. At the bottom, a little spring burst forth, with clear water bubbling up. Coyote built a big fire, heating up rocks. He took his flint knife, cut up the "baby," and threw the pieces into the water. He then threw the rocks in, boiling the meat. He thus showed the people how they would cook when the world came to be. He lay out green twigs, leaves, and grass, and then put the meat out to cool.

Then he called for the other three wicked ones to come to the feast. They started to go, but became suspicious, noticing that one of them was missing. Coyote called again, this time imitating the voice of the dead monster. The others finally came, although they were suspicious.

Coyote just told them, "Here I have all this meat, and I thought you might be hungry."

They had been without game for a while, so they just dug in. One asked Coyote if he had seen the missing one.

Coyote just said, "No," which left them suspicious.

Then one of them realized he was eating a forearm, and that it was the missing one. He screamed. Coyote took out his war club. The monsters ran, screaming, "He's going to kill us!" But Coyote was far too quick, and dispatched them all with the club.

Then Coyote returned to the pool, and said, "From this time forward there will be no wicked ones disguised as babies, and this spring of hot water will be here to heal all generations to come."

This hot spring, made by Coyote, is now private property and off limits to the public. Salish elder Agnes Vanderburg told that when non-Indians built a dirt road through the narrow canyon leading to Snetetšé, they destroyed the rock formation of the Sleeping Child. Some say it was the Sleeping Child's cradle that was cut in half by the road.

Salish elder Eneas Vanderburg at Snetetšé, 1998.

Snk'ʷɫxʷexʷemí

Translation: Place Where They Would Lift Something.

Linguistic analysis: *Es k'ʷɫxʷʔem* means he or she is lifting it. *Snk'ʷɫxʷexʷemí* adds the locative prefix *sn* and reduplication of the verb, meaning a place where something is lifted many times, or customarily.

English name or description: Darby area.

About this placename: Snk'ʷɫxʷexʷemí was a major camp for the Salish near the southern end of the open part of the Bitterroot Valley.

The name *Snk'ʷɫxʷexʷemí* refers to a rock in the Darby area that sat along a trail often used by the Salish. The elders have told of how people would stop along the trail and try to move the rock. Sometimes big, strong men couldn't budge it, but smaller people moved it easily. The people would bet on who could move it the furthest. But it is said that when they would return to the spot, the rock would always be back in its previous location. It is said that non-Indians later destroyed this rock trying to find out what made it move around.

At Snk'ʷɫxʷexʷemí, October 2003: Michael Louis Durglo Sr., Josephine Quequesah, Felicite Sapiel McDonald, Shirley Trahan, Sadie Peone.

Snʔam̓šá

Translation: A Trail Frequently Used for Moving Camp Back and Forth.

Linguistic analysis: *Es ʔim̓ši* means to move camp; with the locative prefix *sn*, *Snʔam̓šá* refers to a trail where people moved camp back and forth all the time.

English name or description: The main trail up the West Fork of the Bitterroot River, leading toward the Selway River in Idaho.

About this placename: Like *Naptnišá* (the Lolo trail), *Snʔam̓šá* was an important and ancient route linking Salish and Nez Perce territories and people.

The West Fork and "Nez Perce" Fork were in themselves areas of great importance to the Salish. In certain spots, the people went to dig bitterroot of enormous size. This was also an abundant hunting area. Near the pass at the top of Snʔam̓šá, Salish hunters often used deer blinds to take as many deer as they might need. Elders remember stories of people taking one hundred deer in a day in this way. The elders also knew this area to abound in *skʷiskʷs* (ruffed grouse).

As recently as the 1940s, Salish people were born along Snʔam̓šá while their families were camping there on fall hunting trips. It is still an important hunting area for members of the Confederated Salish and Koo-tenai Tribes. The Hellgate treaty of 1855 guaranteed the tribal use of this area, like all public lands in the aboriginal territory, for hunting, fishing, and other traditional purposes.

Salish elder Eneas Vanderburg on Snʔam̓šá, 1998.

Čq̓Ѐé

Translation: Where the Ram's Head Got Stuck.

Linguistic analysis: From the Salish word for wedging something into something else; čq̓ʔentén means I wedged something into it.

English name or description: The Medicine Tree.

About this placename: In 2001, an ancient tree fell in the south end of the Bitterroot Valley. This was a sacred tree whose origins lay in the doings of Coyote when he traveled across this land. Many elders would remark that they knew the Coyote stories as far south as Čq̓Ѐé, but no further.

The story that follows draws from what was told by some elders. Like all Coyote stories, this one varies among storytellers in minor details.

As Snčl̓é (Coyote) continued on his journey through what is now called the Bitterroot Valley, he saw his friend W̓ew̓í (Meadowlark) sitting in a bush. Meadowlark remembered that earlier, Coyote had inadvertently stepped on Meadowlark's leg and broken it. But Coyote, who was the first great medicine man, had then fixed a splint for Meadowlark's leg and healed it.

Meadowlark told Coyote that he was sitting in the bush to be out of Coyote's way.

Coyote laughed. He didn't blame Meadowlark for not wanting his leg broken again.

Meadowlark then warned Coyote of a gigantic, mean bighorn sheep ram up ahead, near the south end of the Bitterroot Valley. Ram killed everything that tried to pass.

Coyote thanked Meadowlark and continued on his way. He thought about what Meadowlark had told him and wondered how he could survive this. But Coyote knew that he had to face Ram and kill it to make this place safe for the human beings who were yet to come.

Coyote walked on, and soon he heard a fierce sound. He looked up and saw Ram up on top of the hill. Ram immediately snorted and charged down toward Coyote.

Coyote waited until Ram got very close and then yelled out, "Hold on there!"

Ram was surprised by this and stopped.

Coyote demanded to know why Ram intended to kill him.

Ram replied that it was his place and that for many years he had killed everyone who tried to pass. Coyote knew that in the world to come, although different nations and animals were to have their territories, it would not be acceptable to kill everyone who simply passed through one's land. This monster had to be destroyed.

So Coyote then asked Ram how he killed.

Ram said, "With my powers—I am quick and strong, and my horns are sharp."

Coyote asked Ram to demonstrate this power.

Ram scoffed and said Coyote was just wasting his time.

Coyote then pointed to a little tree and said he wanted to see Ram knock it over.

Ram couldn't resist this easy chance to show his strength. He thundered toward the tree and smashed it with his great head. One horn penetrated all the way through the tree, with the horn sticking out the other side.

Coyote leapt up and grabbed the protruding tip with all his might in one hand, and with the other, pulled out his flint knife. Ram pleaded for his life, but Coyote knew what he had to do, and cut off Ram's head with three swift strokes of the knife.

Coyote then stood by the tree and said, "In the generations of human beings to come, there will be no such wicked creatures. This tree will be a place for human beings to leave offerings of their prized possessions, and to give thanks, and to pray for their well-being, for good fortune and good health. Those who are not sincere and serious in making their wishes will have misfortune and even death."

Then Coyote cut the head of Ram completely away from the horns, and hurled it up on the rocky hillside where it left the profile of a human face. Coyote said, "That face will be a sign of my doings here."

Although the tree fell in 2001, the site remains of sacred importance to Salish and Pend d'Oreille people. We will always return here to pray and give thanks.

Above: *Salish-Pend d'Oreille pilgrimage to Čq̓ʔé, c. 1986.*

Right: *Salish pilgrimage to Čq̓ʔé, 1923.* Left to right: *Adele Vanderburg, Harriet Adams (Whitworth), Mary Kaltomee (Sackwoman), Ateline Joscum, Angelique Finley, Chief Martin Charlo, Eneas Finley, Victor Vanderburg, Rose Marengo.* On the ground: *Louie Pellew.*

K̓ʷtíɫ P̓up̓x̣m̓

Translation: Big Open or Big Clear Area.

Linguistic analysis: *K̓ʷtíɫ*=large, big; *P̓up̓x̣m̓*=emerging from something enclosed into something open.

English name or description: Ross's Hole, on the East Fork of the Bitterroot River, and the open area near the confluence of Camp Creek and the East Fork, near the present town of Sula, Montana.

About this placename: "Our people were camped in a kind of prairie along the Bitterroot River, a few miles upstream from the Medicine Tree," recalled tribal elder Pete Pichette in telling the story of the Salish encounter with the Lewis and Clark expedition. "The place is called Ross's Hole now; the Indians then called it Cutl-kkh-pooh." *Cutl-kkh-pooh* was the transcriber's attempt to represent the name K̓ʷtíɫ P̓u, the truncated version of the placename K̓ʷtíɫ P̓up̓x̣m̓.

K̓ʷtíɫ P̓up̓x̣m̓ was known to the Salish for its excellent horse pasture, for berries and chokecherries, for hunting, and as a camp on the way to the Salmon River country, where they would go to get salmon.

K̓ʷtíɫ P̓up̓x̣m̓ lies along the route sometimes taken to buffalo by the Salish. It is situated along the trail from the Bitterroot Valley to the relatively gentle pass—now called Chief Joseph's Pass—that crosses the Continental Divide and leads into Sk̓ʷumcné, the Big Hole Valley. Buffalo were once numerous in the Big Hole Valley. From there it was an easy journey to places where buffalo once covered the plains, for the Big Hole River drains into the Jefferson, which leads to Three Forks and the Missouri River. Or we could travel farther east toward the Yellowstone Valley. Although K̓ʷtíɫ P̓up̓x̣m̓ lies within traditional Salish territory, it was also an area used by Nez Perce and Shoshone people, whose territories bordered and overlapped the Salish to the west, south, and southeast. For all of these reasons, K̓ʷtíɫ P̓up̓x̣m̓ was a good place for the allied western nations to gather for the buffalo hunts. And in fact, there were some Nez Perce present in the Salish camp at K̓ʷtíɫ P̓up̓x̣m̓ in September 1805.

Above: *Felicite Sapiel McDonald, Margaret Finley, Michael Louis Durglo Sr., and Rae Lynn Charlo at Kʷtíɫ Ṗupʎ̇m̓, July 2002. East Fork Bitterroot River in background.*

Right: *John Peter Paul, September 1998, along Camp Creek with Kʷtíɫ Ṗupʎ̇m̓ (Ross's Hole) in background.*

Skʷumcné Sewɫkʷs

Translation: Waters of the Pocket Gopher.

Linguistic analysis: *Skʷumcné* draws from the word *skʷum̓cn*, a pocket gopher. This word in turn draws upon the verb for storing or caching something away (*es kʷm̓cní* means you're caching something). *Sewɫkʷ* is the word for water; the suffix *s* is a possessive.

English name or description: The Big Hole River (and valley).

About this placename: Long ago—before intertribal relations and territories were altered by the introduction of horses, epidemic diseases, and firearms—the Big Hole was the headquarters for one of the five or six original main bands of the Salish people. It is said that the two largest bands were based at Skʷumcné and Čɫmlšé (the Helena area). In later years, Skʷumcné remained of importance to the Salish for hunting and for gathering many foods and medicines. Elders have told how hunting parties would sometimes run into the Snúwe (Shoshone) in this area; sometimes they would fight each other, and sometimes they were at peace. Skʷumcné was another area where buffalo were once numerous. Before the time of horses, the Salish hunted them in this area on foot.

In this brief tour of a small part of the Salish and Pend d'Oreille lands traversed by the Lewis and Clark expedition in 1805–6, we can begin to see the ancientness of this cultural landscape, and the depth of its meaning for our people. And we can better understand how invisible our world was to the visitors. For all of Lewis and Clark's wonderfully detailed observations of our territory, of plants and animals and overt cultural artifacts, there was just as much that they could not see. And as we will discover in Part 2 of this volume, that current of misunderstanding ran through much of the interaction between our people and the strangers who passed through our country two centuries ago.

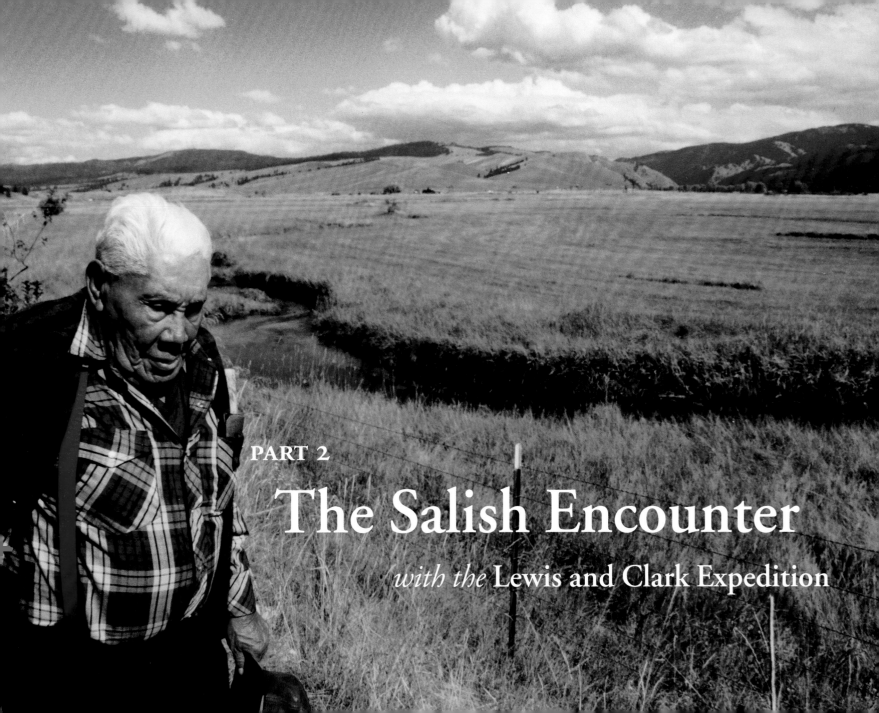

PART 2

The Salish Encounter

with the Lewis and Clark Expedition

The Beginning
of the Great Changes

Horses, Epidemics, and Guns

In part 1, we saw that in 1805, when Lewis and Clark made their way to the homeland of the Salish and Pend d'Oreille people, they entered into an ancient and richly developed cultural world. Yet they also entered a world already in the midst of tremendous change.

In the century preceding the arrival of the expedition, the Salish and Pend d'Oreille were deeply affected by three products of Euro-American society: horses, infectious diseases, and firearms. All arrived in the territory of the *sqélixʷ* well in advance of white people themselves. These three factors forever changed the tribal landscape, altering tribal populations, tribal ways of life, tribal territories, and intertribal relations. Western Montana in 1805 was still a Salish world. But it was a Salish world vastly different from the one that had existed in 1705, 1605, or 1505.

Sometime between about 1650 and 1730, the Salish acquired horses, which gave them much greater mobility and easier access to buffalo and other foods and materials. Horses also made it easier and faster to travel into the territory of other tribes—both friends and enemies. And horses themselves were a newly mobile unit of wealth, prestige, and power. Once stolen, they not only could be transported quickly—they *were* the transportation. As a result, with horses came a dramatic increase in all kinds of contact between tribes, including peaceful exchange and also conflict and warfare.

Despite these changes, Salish and Pend d'Oreille people still lived by the same seasonal cycle of life, ate the same foods, and had the same kind of social organization. Horses were readily adopted by the tribes because the people were able to integrate them fully into the preexisting traditional way of life. The acquisition of horses facilitated and supported, rather than overturned, the fundamental structure and values of Salish and Pend d'Oreille society. This is true even though the introduction of horses was soon followed by devastating cycles of deadly epidemics.

Tribal people had little or no immunity against these new diseases. Archaeologists have found some evidence suggesting that the deadliest of all the European diseases, smallpox, may have swept through the Salishan tribes of the Northwest and decimated native populations as early as the 1500s, long before the first appearance of horses. That epidemic, if it happened, would have started with the conquistadors in Mexico and spread northward through intertribal contact. In any case, it is clear that after horses were here, repeated epidemics struck the various tribes of the Northwest throughout the eighteenth and nineteenth centuries. Horses helped spread disease because they brought a general increase in intertribal contact. In the era of foot travel, infected people might have died before reaching another village or camp, but speeding along on horseback, the ill often survived long enough to unwittingly spread their sickness to others.

It is hard to know exactly how many people died, but it is clear that the numbers were overwhelming. Historical demographers estimate that from about 1780 to 1805—the twenty-five years immediately preceding the arrival of Lewis and Clark—at least half and possibly more than two-thirds of the native people of our region died from introduced diseases. Oral histories tell of particular bands from which only a single person survived.

Before inroduced diseases, there were tens of thousands of Salish and Pend d'Oreille people living in the area now encompassed by western Montana, northern Idaho, and eastern Washington. The likely numbers were far greater than scholars have assumed until very recently. In fact, the pre-disease Salish and Pend d'Oreille population was probably greater than the non-Indian population that inhabited the tribes' aboriginal territories before completion of the transcontinental railroad in 1883. But by the time Lewis and Clark arrived in 1805, a one-time Salish and Pend d'Oreille population that perhaps numbered between twenty-thousand and sixty-thousand had been reduced to an estimated population of between two-thousand and eight-thousand.[1]

In short, a small fraction of the original tribal population remained to witness the arrival of Euro-American people. There were far fewer people here to defend tribal territories against the incursions that soon followed the expedition. Those who had survived lived in tribal bands that were doubtless still deeply affected by the emotional, spiritual, social, and economic effects of the pandemics.

In addition to horses and disease, the introduction of firearms changed the intertribal world. While Lewis and Clark were the first non-Indian visitors to the Bitterroot Valley, and the first whites to have been seen by most of the Salish, at least some tribal people in 1805 knew of white people some days travel to the north. Both the Salish oral tradition told by Mary Kaltomee (Sackwoman, ca. 1845–1957) to elder Louis Adams (b. 1933) and the journal of expedition member Joseph Whitehouse note that some of the Salish people had already seen *ipiq sqélix*ʷ (white people) somewhere in the north country (*ċaltúlex*ʷ).[2] These were probably trappers, voyageurs, and traders associated with the Hudson's Bay Company, which had operated in western Canada since the mid-nineteenth century, or the North West Company, which in 1799 established Rocky Mountain House at the eastern foot of the Rocky Mountains near present-day Red Deer, Alberta. Since at least 1780, when the Hudson's Bay Company established Buckingham House on the Saskatchewan River, the Blackfeet, who were the principal tribal adversaries of the Salish and Pend d'Oreille, had ready access to firearms. For the following thirty to forty years, Salish and Pend d'Oreille warriors were at a great disadvantage in battles with the Blackfeet. After 1810, when fur trading posts were established in Salish-Pend d'Oreille territory, we were able to acquire sufficient firearms to overcome our disadvantage.

However, before 1810, the Salish and Pend d'Oreille were forced to make major territorial changes. As noted earlier in this volume, the tribes originally occupied nearly as much land east of the Continental Divide as west of it. The Salish were organized in five or six major bands, based in areas that included Čxʷtxʷtpé (the Three Forks area), Čɫmlšé (Helena), and Skʷumcné (the Big Hole Valley). With the onset of the epidemics, the presence of horses, and the destabilizing effect of guns, the Blackfeet swept into the northern Montana plains, pushing other tribes out. The Plains Shoshone were forced south and west, and the Plains bands of Salish, Pend d'Oreille, and Kootenai moved their winter camps west across the mountains. The western tribes continued to use their ancestral buffalo hunting grounds east of the mountains, but with the constant threat of Blackfeet raids, we could no longer live there permanently. By the time Lewis and Clark arrived, the territorial transition had already occurred.

During this important period in tribal history—the late eighteenth and early nineteenth centuries—the Salishan and Sahaptin peoples developed a strategy to increase their safety while hunting buffalo in areas near the larger and better-armed Blackfeet. The western tribes would gather together, forming large multitribal hunting parties as they ventured east across the mountains for buffalo. The journals of the Lewis and Clark expedition note that there were some Nez Perce present among the Salish at Kʷtiɫ Ṗupx̣m̓ in September 1805, as the group prepared to head east for the fall hunt. The journals also noted that the Shoshone were on their way to buffalo at this same time. Later in the nineteenth century, many non-Indian visitors and fur trappers described great buffalo hunting parties comprised of Salish, upper and lower Pend d'Oreille, Nez Perce, Spokane, Coeur d'Alene, Colville, Kootenai, Shoshone, and other tribes.

Some historians have given us the impression that change—even history itself—only began in the Rocky Mountains with the arrival of Lewis and Clark. In part 1, we saw that human history in our region predated the expedition by thousands of years. And here, in the history of horses, diseases, and guns, we see that even the cataclysmic changes in Indian society that we usually associate with the arrival of non-Indians actually began well before Lewis and Clark. The Salish and Pend d'Oreille, in short, were already in a state of considerable upheaval by 1805. Little did our ancestors realize that Lewis and Clark's brief visit would initiate an even more traumatic and devastating cycle of change.

The Question of Intent

*Salish Perspectives on the Purpose
of the Lewis and Clark Expedition*

In his original instructions to Meriwether Lewis, President Thomas Jefferson clearly stated the purpose of the expedition: "The object of your mission," wrote Jefferson, "is to explore the Missouri river," and to find the best water route to the Pacific Ocean, "for the purposes of commerce." And when Jefferson wrote to Congress seeking funding for the expedition, the president mentioned scientific inquiry as merely "incidental" and "an additional gratification." Although Jefferson held a deep, personal interest in the project's strictly exploratory and scientific goals, the law subsequently passed by Congress was entitled "An Act making an appropriation for extending the external commerce of the United States."[1] In short, Lewis and Clark were primarily sent west to lay the groundwork for the development of an American fur trade in the newly acquired lands of the Louisiana Purchase.

Both Jefferson and the Congress knew that despite the supposed "sale" of that land, neither France nor the United States actually controlled or held legitimate title to the western half of the continent. Furthermore, Jefferson noted, most native nations were adamantly

Left: Salish Scouts. *Oil painting by
Tony Sandoval, 2003.*

opposed to any further cessions of land. "The policy has long been gaining strength with them," he wrote in his confidential message to Congress in January 1803, "of refusing absolutely all further sale [of land] on any conditions." Jefferson explained to Congress that the expedition could help to change that. He argued that the establishment of American trading posts would not only help offset the influence of the British Hudson's Bay Company, but would also help turn Indian people away from their traditional ways of life, toward the agricultural and commercial economic system. Jefferson thought that pulling the western tribes into the American economy and way of life would, in turn, reduce their need for large tracts of land, and thus reduce their opposition to selling it.[2] The larger purpose of the Lewis and Clark expedition then, beyond the expansion of the American fur trade, was to take control of native lands from native peoples.

The real intents and purposes of the expedition are clear to any disinterested reader of the papers surrounding the expedition. But few of these material aims appeared in the message that William Clark and

Meriwether Lewis delivered either to the Salish or to the other tribes along their route. Among the Salish, Lewis and Clark may have kept their speeches even shorter and less fully truthful than usual, because of the particularly cumbersome translation problems. According to the journals, they didn't say much at all to the Salish until their second day at Kʷtł̱ Ṗupᵻ̓m̓, after a night of smoking and eating together, and listening to the speeches of Salish leaders. Private Joseph Whitehouse's journal notes that Lewis and Clark "told them that we could not Stop long with them and that we were ready to purchase their horses, and that we could not talk with them as much as we wish, for all that we Say has to go through 6 languages before it gits to them and it is hard to make them understand all what we Say." When they did talk, according to Whitehouse, they told the Salish "nearly the same as they told other nations, only told them we wanted a fiew horses from them, and we would give them Some merchandize in return." Clark says "we informed them where we Came from, where bound and for what purpose &c. &c. and requested to purchase & exchange a fiew horses with them." Sergeant Ordway said "our officers made four chiefs gave them meddles 2 flags Some other Small presents and told them our business and that we were friends to all the red people &c. which they appeared verry friendly to us."[3]

Given Lewis and Clark's rosy—and brief—presentation, the Salish were naturally unaware of the expedition's full objectives, and so we gave the visitors a great deal of help during their brief encounter. The white men's stock was exhausted, and so our people gave them a dozen "ellegant horses," as Clark described them. In return, the Salish graciously accepted seven lame animals and a few small gifts. The tribe also gave the strangers food from their dried stores, robes, and a dozen pack saddles—altogether, goods representing a very great amount of labor, primarily the work of Salish women over countless days and months. The gifts were the products of strenuous, exacting work: hunting, processing the animals, brain-tanning hides, sewing them, gathering and drying and storing foods, constructing saddles, and transporting all these materials.

The Salish were not trading, but engaging in gift-giving, as was customary in providing a proper welcome to new guests. The expedition members seemed not to fully understand the generosity of the Salish and thought they had somehow managed to bargain their way to a good deal. Clark wrote that "the cheap rate at which horses are to be obtained from the Indians of the Rocky Mountains and west of them reduce the expences of transportation over this portage [across the Bitterroots] to a mere trifle."[4] Clark must have felt he was remarkably fortunate, for, as he admitted, the party had not "met with any of the nativs of the Rocky Mountains" prior to reaching the Shoshones, and therefore "were of course ignorant of the passes by land which existed through those mountains to the Columbia river, and had we even known the rout we were destitute of horses which would have been indispendibly necessary to enable us to transport the requisit quantity of amunition and other stores to ensure the success of the remaining part of our voyage down the Columbia."[5]

The horses that the Salish gave to Lewis and Clark may have saved the lives of at least some members of the expedition. When the strangers left the Salish at Kʷtíɫ P̓upx̣m̓, they proceeded north through the Bitterroot Valley until they reached Lolo Creek, where they turned west and moved on toward Idaho, over the Bitterroot Mountains along Naptnišá (the Lolo Trail). They and their elderly Shoshone guide didn't know the trail well, and they moved slowly through deep snows and bitter cold. For over a week, they were forced to subsist on the meat of the Salish horses. As Lewis wrote after his return, *"most fortunately on our way within the Mountains we met with a travelling Band of the Tushopahs [Salish] going to the Plains of the Missesourii in quest of Buffaloe & obtained from them an accession of 7 Horses to our former Stock exchanging at the same time 10 or 12 to great advantage; this ultimately proved of infinite Service to us as we were compelled to subsist on Horse Beef & Dogs previous to our arrival in the navigable [part] of the Kooskooskee [Clearwater River]. I have not the leisure at this moment to state all those difficulties which we encountered in our Passage over these Mountains—suffice it to say we suffered everything Cold, Hunger, & Fatigue could impart, or the Keenest Anxiety excited for the fate of the Expedition in which our whole Souls were embarked."*[6]

In later years, the Salish and many other tribes would discover the real purpose of the expedition—the assertion of dominion over Indian lands and Indian peoples, and the commercial exploitation of Indian resources. In a famous speech printed in 1876 by Montana newspapers, the Head Chief of the Bitterroot Salish from 1870 to 1910, Słm̓x̣e Q̓oxʷqeys (Claw of the Small Grizzly Bear, or Chief Charlo), bitterly expressed this profound sense of betrayal, of how tribal people had their kindnesses repaid with injustice and impoverishment. Although the speech does not mention Lewis and Clark by name, it refers directly to the ways the Salish welcomed the expedition—but were deceived as to the party's true intentions. The speech reads in part:

Since our forefathers first beheld him . . . [the whiteman] has filled graves with our bones. . . . His course is destruction. He spoils what the Spirit who gave us this country made beautiful and clean. But that is not enough. He wants us to pay him besides his enslaving our country . . . and . . . that degradation of a Tribe who never were his enemies. What is he? Who sent him here? We were happy when he first came. . . . To take and to lie should be burned on his forehead, as he burns the sides of my horses with his own name. Had heaven's Chief burnt him with some mark, we might have refused him. No, we did not refuse him in his weakness. In his poverty we fed, we cherished him—yes, befriended him, and showed the fords and defiles of our lands. . . .

We owe him nothing. He owes us more than he will pay. . . .

His laws never gave us a blade of grass nor a tree nor a duck nor a grouse nor a trout. . . . You know that he comes as long as he lives, and takes more and more, and dirties what he leaves.[7]

Charlot.

Selish. 5.

The anger expressed by Chief Charlo over the general history of white invasion, and his sense that the Lewis and Clark expedition exploited the hospitality of Indian people, are also reflected in a story told by Salish elder Bud Barnaby. In the 1930s Chief Charlo's grandson, Tony Charlo, who himself would later serve our people as chief, was on a fire-fighting crew working on the Wind River Reservation in Wyoming, home to Shoshone and Arapaho people. The crew was camped next to a cemetery at Fort Washakie. Tony noticed that all of the graves—including the graves of numerous Salish people who had lived among the Shoshone—were kept clean and tidy, except one, which was covered with weeds and tall grass. Tony asked some of the Shoshone firefighters to explain this. They told him that it was the grave of Sacajawea, who had shown the white men their country. Today this animus is gone. Out of compassion and respect for Sacajawea, and out of consideration for her descendants, the grave is now well tended.[8]

Right: Chief Charlo (S✝m̓x̣e Q̓oxʷqeys), *1884.*

89

To Help Them
or to Wipe Them Out

*Stories of Misunderstanding
and Miscommunication*

Most histories and films of the Lewis and Clark expedition have depicted their encounters with Indian people as, in general, a story of respectful cultural exchange and mutual understanding—a model of peaceful interaction. Those mainstream accounts of Lewis and Clark tend to portray Indian-white conflict and injustices committed against native people as something that only happened in later years—as if those conflicts and injustices were an unfortunate deviation from the noble precedent set by the explorers.

But when we listen to the elders' stories, or even when we carefully read some of the expedition's own journals, the meetings between Lewis and Clark and native people were marked primarily by misunderstanding and miscommunication. We have already noted the difficulty of the translation process. Joseph Whitehouse said the expedition members found the Salish language very difficult, so they figured the Salish must be the

Left: Čeɫl Sq̓eẏmí (Chief Three Eagles), elders, and warriors discuss whether the expedition poses a threat to the tribe. Oil painting by Tony Sandoval, 2003.

"Welsh Indians," drawing on an old myth about a group of Welsh people who had supposedly sailed to North America and settled on the upper Missouri. As the expedition members struggled to understand languages and cultures that were utterly foreign to them, they naturally drew on their own mythologies.

Clearly, there was misunderstanding on both sides. As the elders have told us, the Salish thought the expedition members must have been in mourning, since their hair was cut short. They thought their skin was pale pink in color because they were cold. They thought the African American member of the expedition, York, was a warrior who had painted himself black in preparation for war, or in mourning after his defeat in battle. Or perhaps he was a q̓ʷásq̓ʷiʔ—a ceremonial blue jay, with his face covered in charcoal. Elders tell of how Salish people approached York and dabbed their fingers on his face to see if the black color would rub off. From this encounter came the gesture in tribal sign language for an African American person—dabbing one's cheek with an index finger.

As we can see, the accounts of tribal elders and non-Indians alike reflect the confusion in these interactions. But there is also a crucial difference in how these stories are told. The Salish accounts consciously *focus* on the misunderstanding. They make a point of how Indians misinterpreted the white visitors, and of how the white men also misunderstood their Salish hosts. In contrast, most mainstream accounts of the expedition, with some prominent exceptions, downplay or even deny Lewis and Clark's profound misunderstanding of the native peoples they encountered during their journey. Most of these accounts minimize, or treat as a curious side issue, the expedition members' inability to communicate very well with Indians, including the Salish.

Why is there this great difference in the stories? Perhaps, by obscuring the misunderstanding and miscommunication so prevalent in the meeting, mainstream accounts perpetuate the myth that Indian people welcomed the explorers in the full knowledge of their intentions. Many of those widely popularized stories direct our attention away from seriously considering that this was the first step of an unprovoked invasion of the sovereign territory of other peoples. In doing so, they manage to preserve the romantic glow of the Corps of Discovery myth—the sense that this was, at heart, a morally right undertaking, and that native people then, or readers today, could have no serious objection to what Lewis and Clark were doing.

The elders' stories, on the other hand, suggest that the very survival of the expedition was the product of Salish misunderstanding. As the elders make clear, the first decision of the chief, Čełł Sq̓ey̓mí, (Three Eagles), was to determine whether the strange party constituted a threat to the people's well-being—that is, whether they should be welcomed or wiped out. Even Pete Pichette's account, which as translated says the chief "immediately" told the warriors to bring the strangers into camp and "do no harm to them," implicitly reflects that Chief Three Eagles at least briefly considered another option: treating the strangers as hostile intruders and having the men go after them.[1] By Lewis's reckoning, the Salish had a force of about eighty warriors at K̓ʷtiłł P̓up̓ṁ. Fortunately for the expedition, Chief Three Eagles reached the conclusion that the strangers were not a threat. But the elders all say that Three Eagles based his decision on mistaken guesses as to the reason for York's dark color. Although the strangers appeared to be a war party, they also seemed pitiful and perhaps in mourning.

The Salish leader had no way to know of President Jefferson's instructions, no way to know of the real purpose of the expedition, no way to know of the vast expansionist ambitions of U.S. officials and their hunger for the lands and resources that belonged to the Salish and other Indian people. As Pete Beaverhead said, the Salish "believed and trusted" in their gifts and their words of friendship. And so they fed the visitors and supplied them with life-saving horses.

"The chief immediately sent his warriors to meet the strange men and bring them to camp safely."

Pete Pichette *via* Ella Clark

Right: *Trying to translate across languages and cultures. Oil painting by Tony Sandoval, 2003.*

Our people were camped in a kind of prairie along the Bitterroot River, a few miles upstream from the Medicine Tree. The place is called Ross's Hole now; the Indians then called it Cutl-kkh-pooh. They kept close watch over their camps in those days and always had scouts out because they feared an attack by an enemy tribe. One day two scouts came back to report that they had seen some human beings who were very different from any they had known. Most of the strangers had pale skins, and their clothing was altogether different from anything the Indians wore.

"There were seven of them," the scouts told Chief Three Eagles [pronounced *Tchliska-e-mee* in Salish].

"I think they have had a narrow escape from their

enemies. All their belongings were taken away by the enemy. That's why there is so little in their packs. Maybe the rest of the tribe were killed. Maybe that is why there are only seven of them. These men must be very hungry, perhaps starving. And see how poor and torn their clothes are." The chief ordered food to be brought to them—dried buffalo meat and dried roots. He ordered clothing also to be brought to them—buckskins and light buffalo robes that were used for clothing.

One of the strange men was black. He had painted himself in charcoal, my people thought. In those days it was the custom for warriors, when returning home from battle, to prepare themselves before reaching camp. Those who had been brave and fearless, the victorious ones in battle, painted themselves in charcoal. When the warriors returned to their camp, people knew at once which ones had been brave on the warpath. So the black man, they thought, had been the bravest of this party.

All the men had short hair. So our people thought that the seven were in mourning for the rest of the party who had been slaughtered. It was the custom for mourners to cut their hair.

By signs, Chief Three Eagles and his counselors came to a little understanding with the white men. Then the chief said to his people, "This party is the first of this kind of people we have ever seen. They have been brought in safely. I want them taken out safely. I want you warriors to go with them part of the way to make sure that they leave our country without harm."

So by the chief's orders, a group of young warriors accompanied the white men to the edge of the Salish country. They went with the strangers down the river from Ross's Hole and up to Lolo Pass. The white men went on from there.

They did not take with them the robes and clothing Chief Three Eagles had given them. Perhaps the white men did not understand that they were gifts.

Left: *The Salish meet the expedition party. Oil painting by Tony Sandoval, 2003.*

Right: Kʷtíⱡ Pupⱡm *(Ross's Hole) in the 1920s.*

"She said they were concerned when they saw them, because they had a qʷásq̓ʷiʔ with them."

Louie Adams

What I'll tell about is what I heard from Sophie Moiese. She was my grandma—Louise Vanderburg's step-mom. She used to visit us a lot in the wintertime. My folks used to go after her sometimes—she'd stay with us for a week or two—to tell Coyote stories. And they just enjoyed her. She was a nice old lady. And that was after she'd lost [her husband] Victor [Vanderburg], in 1939. . . .

But I heard her tell about her folks, or her grandparents—whoever it was that encountered Lewis and Clark in the Bitterroot. She said these strangers came—from whichever direction they came from, these *suyapis* [white people]. She said they were really concerned when they saw them, she said, because they had a *qʷásqʷiʔ* with them.

A $q^{w}\acute{a}sq^{w}i\mathfrak{2}$ to our people is a bluejay. For thousands of years, we have had medicine dances every winter. . . . In the old days, I guess there was quite a lot of them. And these were the people who would blacken their faces with coals. They had an important role in the medicine dances, because they were smart people.

And when they saw this, this $q^{w}\acute{a}sq^{w}i\mathfrak{2}$ with Lewis and Clark—these pale people—they wondered what kind of ceremony there was going to be, what they were up to. Because without this black man, they probably would have just welcomed them into their camp, and fed them, so these people could be on their way. They were a little bit leery of them when they seen this black man.

And through the course of communication—with this sign language—they had a rough time, but eventually they got across to Lewis and Clark that they wanted to know why they had a black man with them, a $q^{w}\acute{a}sq^{w}i\mathfrak{2}$.

And Lewis or Clark, whichever one, finally told them that this was not a bluejay, that he was a black man, that it was his natural color.

So, a lot of our people, Sophie Moiese used to say, a lot of them went up to this black man and rubbed their finger on his face to see if any of it would come off. It didn't! So then they were convinced that it was a black man, it was his natural color.

And that's why in our sign language, when you talk about a black person, you're telling somebody you saw a black man, you'd say, "I saw a $\dot{q}^{w}y\acute{o}s$," just by sign language, you'd rub a finger on your face. . . .

After that, I guess they relaxed, and then they realized they weren't up to—of course, they *were* up to something, but they didn't. . . . [chuckles]

They was thinking [about the question of whether] it was something imminently dangerous to them, you know, at first. . . .

And then I was invited to Hamilton last year. I've been invited up there two years in a row to talk with the Chamber of Commerce. . . . And when I got up to talk, I said, "Yes, Flatheads is a misnomer. We *are Séliš* [Salish]." I said, "And also, Oot-la-shoots is a misnomer." I said, "We're not that." I said, . . . "I studied it over a few days, and I thought, by golly, I'll bet Three Eagles, when he met with these people, they asked in sign language, 'Where do you people live?' And if they were way up at Ross Hole somewhere, he probably just pointed down below toward Hamilton, toward what is now Hamilton, Stevensville, and he said, '*Tl' išút.*' So the whiteman wrote, 'Oot-la-shoot.' And all it means, *tl' išút*, is 'down below.' ". . . .

And our old people used to talk about Sk^{w}tíł X̣q^{w}ólex^{w}, back there someplace. This, I don't know whether it was Big Hole, or Ross Hole—wherever, I don't know. But I used to hear this once in a while when they'd talk about the Bitterroot. Sk^{w}tíł X̣q^{w}ólex^{w}. Which means like a big prairie, you know. . . .

I heard her [Mary Kaltomee, or Sackwoman] say that a few times—that Lewis and Clark were not the first white people that *some* of our Indians had encountered. She was probably talking about her folks, or grandparents—somewhere down the line, she said—"because

some of our people had seen white people *tl̓ čaltúlex^w*—from the north."

So to some of our people, it wasn't a big surprise to see Lewis and Clark. I imagine they all heard about white people. Because you know, if somebody did see some of them from the north, then the story goes around.

Above: Salish and York. *Oil painting by Tony Sandoval, 2003.*

"Sophie Moiese said if it wasn't for York, they would have wiped out that party."

Joe Vanderburg

It's Sophie Moiese's words—I mean, I don't know how else you could tell it.

She said that they were east of the mountains, from what she was told, and they'd had one hell of a fight—I guess with the Blackfeet. Their numbers, their warriors, were decimated.

And they were on their way back to the Bitterroots when they came upon—I don't know if it was Clark's main party or part of it. And York was with the group. There mustn't have been that many of them. It probably was when Clark and Lewis were separated, checking out different drainages and so forth.

And they came upon them, and right at first they were going to attack.

And then someone said, "No, we can't," because they said, "Look, one of them blackened himself." Because that was the custom then—if you were defeated by another, by an enemy, well, you blackened yourself, and it was like a white flag, I guess. And everyone else left you alone.

And then when they did meet this party, they found out that the man was actually black. He didn't blacken himself.

And they said, "Well, you know, there's no use any of us to have another fight, because most of our warriors are gone anyway, and we don't think we could do very well." So that was when they stopped. . . .

[Sophie Moiese] named them, she said there was some hotheads who still wanted to do battle, and some of the rest, some of the older people, I guess, said, "No, just let it go."

She said if it wasn't for York, they would have wiped out that party.

It must not have been a very big party, because I think they split up—part of them went up to, what is it, the Milk River, or Marias River, or somewhere up that way, and then the other one went toward the south. . . . But I guess from what she said, must've been a small party of what they met initially. And later I guess they met the main party. . . . Well then, that group I guess took them to the main party.

Well, after seeing him, they thought . . . "Well, look, there one of them has painted himself black. That's the sign of defeat, and they want no more fighting." And that was when I guess, well, they decided not to do battle. And from there, I guess they went to the main party—I guess Lewis and Clark.

If York hadn't have been with them, they would have wiped out that particular party.

10,000 Years Indigenous People—200 Years Lewis and Clark, number 7a, by Corky Clairmont, 2001.

Gift-giving *and* Confusion

The accounts of Louie Adams and Pete Pichette, and the following story told by Salish elder Sophie Moiese (1864–1960), provide vivid examples of the confusion—and sometimes conflict—that often arose around the exchange of goods between tribal people and the expedition party. Mr. Pichette reports that the expedition members did not take the robes that had been given them. Mrs. Moiese notes that they didn't eat the dried meat and baked camas that was set before them. The story Edward S. Curtis recorded says the white men did not sit on the robes brought to them for that purpose, but instead threw them over their shoulders.

It is a reflection of Mr. Pichette and Mrs. Moiese's generosity of spirit that they both offer charitable explanations for actions that are usually considered highly offensive in tribal culture, especially around the giving of gifts. Mr. Pichette speculates that "perhaps the white men did not understand that they were gifts." Mrs. Moiese offers that they thought the meat "was bark or wood." But of course Lewis and Clark had long since seen most of these foods, including dried meat and berries. It is possible they were suffering from the serious gastrointestinal problems that were a chronic affliction for the expedition members.

Just to the west, among the Nez Perce, another expedition member repeated the same grave insult of refusing food offered in a ceremonial way by a woman. The reaction there was more explosive. According to the journal of Joseph Whitehouse, the woman "took a Sharp flint from hir husband and cut her arms in Sundry places so that the blood gushed out."[1]

"*They didn't know that camas roots are good to eat.*"

Sophie Moiese (Čłxʷm̓xʷm̓šn̓á)
via Louie Pierre and Ella Clark

When the dried meat was brought to the men, they just looked at it and put it back. It was really good to eat, but they seemed to think it was bark or wood.

Also, they didn't know that camas roots are good to eat. . . . Chief Three Eagles told his people that they must not harm the strangers in any way. Since then, no one has ever heard of the Salish tribe and whites getting into battle.

"At a distance he saw a party of about twenty men traveling toward his camp."

Francois Saxa *via* Jerome D'Aste S.J. and Olin D. Wheeler

The Flathead [Salish] Indians were camping at Ross's Hole, or Ross's fork, at the head of the Bitterroot valley, when one day the old chief, Three Eagles, the father of Chief Victor and grandfather of Charlot, left the camp to go scouting the country, fearing there might be some Indian enemies around with the intent to steal horses, as it was done then very frequently. He saw at a distance Lewis and Clark's party, about twenty men, each man leading two pack horses, except two, who were riding ahead, who were Lewis and Clark. The old chief, seeing that these men wore no blankets, did not know what to think of them. It was the first time he had met men without blankets. What kind of beings could they be? The first thought was that they were a party of men who, traveling, had been robbed by some Indians of their blankets. He went back to his people and, reporting to them what he had seen, he gave orders that all the horses should be driven in and watched, for fear the party he had seen might be on a stealing expedition. He then went back toward the party of strange beings, and, hiding himself in the timber, watched them.

When they came to the open prairie he noticed that they traveled slowly and unconcerned, all together, the two leaders going ahead of the party and looking around, as if surveying the country and consulting with their men. He thought within himself: These must be two chiefs; but what can they be after? To make things more complicated for the old chief, there was a colored man in the party. What can this man be? When the Indians were going to the buffalo hunt they had a custom, if any sign would appear of their enemies hiding around, to have a *war dance* to encourage one another to fight and be brave. For this dance, the Indian warriors would paint themselves, some in red, some in yellow, some in black, etc., and from the color each had chosen to paint himself his name was called. The black face, thought the old chief, must surely be a man who painted his face black in sign of war. The party must have had a fight with some hostile Indians and escaped from their enemies, losing only their blankets.

Seeing that the strangers were traveling in the direction of his camp, the old chief went back to his people and told them to keep quiet and wait for the party to come near. From the easy and unconcerned way the strange beings were traveling, the Indians inferred they had no intention to fight or to injure them. Hence, when they saw the strangers advancing, in the same manner, toward them, and were already near their camp, the Indians did not move, but kept watching. When the two leaders of the party, coming to the Indian camp, showed friendship to the Indians, there was a universal shaking of hands. The chief then gave orders to the Indians to bring in the best buffalo hides, one for each man to sit on, and the best buffalo robes also, one for each man to use as a blanket. Then the two leaders, observing that the Indians were using, for smoking, the leaves of some plant, a plant very much alike to our tobacco plant, asked for some and filled their pipes; but as soon as they tried to smoke, they pronounced the *Indian tobacco* no good. Cutting some of their own tobacco they gave it to the Indians, telling them to fill their pipes with it. But it was too much for them, who had never tried the American weed, and all began to cough, with great delight to the party. Then the two leaders asked the Indians for some Kinnickinnick, mixed it with the tobacco, and gave again to the Indians the prepared weed to smoke. This time the Indians found it excellent, and in their way thanked the men whom they now believed a friendly party. On their side the whites, seeing the friendly dispositions of the Indians, decided to camp right there, and they began to unpack their horses, giving the Indians to understand that they also had blankets in their packs, but that they used them only to sleep in, and gave them back the robes. The Indians were soon out of their wits when they saw some of the men packing on their shoulders pretty good sized logs for their camp fires, and conceived a great idea of the power of the white man. All went on friendly, and after

three days they started off, directed to Lolo fork's trail by the Indians, as the best way to go to the Nez Perces' country.

    I am yours respectfully,

    J. D'Aste, S.J.

Above: *Exchanging tobacco. Oil painting by Tony Sandoval, 2003.*

"They wondered at the unseemly trousers, and pityingly gave them blankets to cover their legs . . ."

Old Eugenie *via* Mother Amadeus and Mother Angela Lincoln

Captain Lewis and Captain Clark were . . . the first white men to enter the present limits of the State of Montana. Old Eugenie, who was still living in 1890, when Mother Amadeus opened the Mission at St. Ignatius, remembered the reverence with which the Indians carried on about the first white men they had ever seen, how they wondered at the unseemly trousers, and pityingly gave them blankets to cover their legs before they suffered them to treat with Indian dignitaries. . . .

Old Eugenie, who lived to be one hundred years old . . . told that when Lewis and Clark came, they gave the Flatheads a present of a bell and a looking glass. . . .

"Buffalo skins were brought, but instead of sitting on them, the white men threw them about their shoulders."

Unknown Salish elder *via* Edward S. Curtis

The two captains advanced and shook hands with the chief, who commanded his people to refrain from any evil-doing toward them.

The white men removed the pack-saddles from their horses and sat down on the ground.

The chief said, "They have no robes to sit on. Some Indians have stolen them. Bring them robes."

Buffalo skins were brought, but instead of sitting on them, the white men threw them about their shoulders.

One of their men had a black face, and the Indians said among themselves, "See, his face is painted black! They are going to have a scalp-dance."

"Clarke took unto himself a Flathead woman.
One son was the result of this union."

Oshanee (b. c. 1791) *via* unnamed interpreter and U.S. Indian Agent Peter Ronan

During the stay of the explorers in the Flathead camp Captain Clarke took unto himself a Flathead woman.

One son was the result of this union, and he was baptised after the missionaries came to Bitter Root valley and named Peter Clarke. This halfbreed lived to a ripe age, and was well known to many of Montana's early settlers. He died about six years ago and left a son, who was christened at St. Mary's mission to the name of Zachariah, and pronounced Sacalee by the Indians. The latter has a son three years of age, whom it is claimed by the Indians, in direct descent, to be the great grandson of the renowned Captain Clarke.

Left: *Misunderstanding and miscommunication. Oil painting by Tony Sandoval, 2003.*

This page, left to right: *Mary Clark, granddaughter of William Clark;* center, *her husband;* right, *their daughter, Lucy.*

Overleaf: *Salish guides show the expedition the way toward the Bitterroot Valley. Oil painting by Tony Sandoval, 2003.*

Lewis and Clark *in the* Fold *of* Tribal History

In the account told by Oshanee, written down by Agent Peter Ronan, we learn that an Indian woman later bore a child fathered by William Clark. While the Oshanee/Ronan story says the woman was Salish, the expedition journals suggest she was Nez Perce. Oshanee herself mentions that the Salish and Nez Perce were camped together, on their way to buffalo, when they met Lewis and Clark. Perhaps Clark left behind children in both tribes; or perhaps his son was born among the Nez Perce, but his descendants lived among and intermarried with the Salish, as did many Nez Perce during the nineteenth century. In any case, it is clear that both the Salish and the Nez Perce maintain oral traditions of Clark's descendants. And we know that at least some of those descendants lived on the Flathead Reservation. In fact, evidence of this appears in the archival record nearly ninety years after the Salish hosted the expedition at Kʷtiɫ Pupłm̓, when the commissioner of Indian affairs received a regular monthly report from Agent Ronan. Ronan's report, dated January 4, 1893, reads in part:

Sir:

A young Indian called Sacalee Clarke, the reputed grandson of Captain Clarke, the explorer, was killed at Arlee station, on the reservation, on the night of December 27th [1892], by attempting, it is supposed, to get off the train while in motion. . . .

Very respectfully,

Your obedient servant

Peter Ronan
United States Indian Agent [1]

This brief mention of the death of William Clark's grandson, buried in an obscure document in the National Archives, seems a tragic and telling epilogue to the story of the Salish encounter with Lewis and Clark. Like so many other forgotten aspects of this history, like so many tribal voices and perspectives left out of the books and films about the expedition, so Sacalee Clark has been lost to the past. We know nothing more about him than when and where he died. But we do know that the world he lived in, the tribal community of which he was a part, was shaped in ways large and small by the aftermath of the expedition that his grandfather led into Salish territory.

When William Clark and Meriwether Lewis returned to St. Louis in September 1806, they immediately wrote to President Jefferson. Lewis's letter carried eastward the first information from the expedition, and it focused, most of all, on the potential of the region for a booming American fur trade:

> We view this passage across the Continent as affording immence advantages to the fur trade. . . . The Missouri and all it's branches from the Cheyenne upwards abound more in beaver and Common Otter, than any other streams on earth, particularly that portion of them lying within the Rocky Mountains. . . . Although the Columbia does not as much as the Missouri abound in beaver and Otter . . . it . . . would furnish a valuable fur trade. . . . There might be collected considerable quantities of the skins of three species of bear affording a great variety of colours and of superior delicacy, those also of the tyger cat, several species of fox, martin and several others.[2]

Lewis and Clark failed to publish their journals for years, and so it is questionable whether the information they gathered contributed, as Jefferson had hoped, in a direct way to the American fur trade's colonization of the upper Missouri and Columbia drainages.[3] But whether or not they directly succeeded, there can be no question that the expedition's primary objective was the commercial exploitation of native lands and resources. Lewis and Clark not only laid claim to those resources, but they also opened the way for wider American involvement in the region.

Nevertheless, in succeeding decades, even as the fur trade boomed across the vast Salish-Pend d'Oreille territories, the region still remained ordered by tribal cultures and tribal economies. Some tribes, particularly in Canada, participated intensively in trapping beaver and other animals, but the Salish, Pend d'Oreille, and neighboring tribes had only a sporadic involvement in the industry. The native people of this area continued to control major aspects of economic life within our territories—and so we used the fur trade for our own purposes. The trade we engaged in with non-Indians supplemented, rather than replaced, our traditional way of life. The Salish and Pend d'Oreille accordingly maintained generally peaceful relations with the trappers and traders and intermarried with some, including Peter Skene Ogden of the Hudson's Bay Company.

Yet the journals of many fur traders in areas west of the Continental Divide are also riddled with instances of conflict and confrontation with tribal people, including certain Nez Perce bands who opposed the unsustainable looting of their resources. As the complex ecological effects of the trade rippled across the region, and as the animals that helped sustain the people became ever scarcer, the tribes themselves became poorer and gradually more dependent on the non-Indian economy and way of life. By the 1840s, the height of the fur trade had passed due to the near extermination of so many animals.

Right: *St. Mary's church at Łq̓etml̓š (Stevensville), Bitterroot Valley, c. 1884. The original St. Mary's Mission, built in 1841, was sold by the Jesuits to John Owen in 1850 and turned into a trading post (Fort Owen). The church in this picture, which still stands, was built in the 1860s, when the Jesuits returned to the Bitterroot Salish community.*

At the same time, another element of non-Indian society was being established in the heart of Salish territory. Many years before, a prophetic vision received by a man named X̣all̓qs (Shining Shirt) foretold of strange men in black robes who would teach the people a new way of prayer. Shining Shirt's vision was reinforced by Iroquois who had come west with the fur trade around 1817 and then settled in the Salish community. They told the Salish of the different way of prayer taught by the Blackrobes (Catholic priests) at their home community of Caughnawaga. With continuing raids from the Blackfeet, changing economic and ecological conditions stemming from the fur trade, and repeated losses from epidemics of European diseases, it was a time of increasing trouble for the Salish. Perhaps the power of the Blackrobes could help. During the 1830s, the Salish sent four delegations to St. Louis to seek out the priests. The Jesuits finally responded, and in 1841, in the valley that Lewis and Clark had crossed less than four decades before, the Salish and the Blackrobes together erected a small mission church.

By the late 1840s, the Salish had come to realize that the Jesuits were not interested in merely contributing their religious gifts to the Salish community—in adding their way of prayer to the existing tribal spirituality—but rather in expunging entirely the native beliefs and ceremonies, which they regarded as the "work of the devil." As Lewis and Clark had done a half century earlier, the Blackrobes gave the Salish a false impression of their objectives and their view of native people. In addition, some people felt betrayed by Blackrobes when they established a mission among the enemy Blackfeet. The Salish turned away from the missionaries, who were then left exposed to Blackfeet raids. The Jesuits left the Bitterroot Valley in 1849 and established the first St. Ignatius mission among the Kalispels. In 1854, they returned to Montana to establish the second St. Ignatius mission, at its current location in the Mission Valley. Many Salish and Pend d'Oreille people embraced Catholicism, and since that time, the cultural and spiritual life of many tribal people has consisted of a blend of native and Christian ways.

In the wake of the fur trade and the missionaries, the pace of change only quickened. Beginning in 1854, Isaac Stevens, the new governor and superintendent of Indian affairs for Washington Territory, convened formal treaty negotiations with tribes throughout the present areas of Washington, northern Idaho, and western Montana. His main objective was to gain for the United States formal ownership of vast tribal lands. He aimed to concentrate numerous tribes onto single reservations, thereby clearing the way for non-Indian control and settlement of most areas.

In July 1855, Stevens met with leaders of the Salish, Pend d'Oreille, and Kootenai at a place we call Člmé, just west of Missoula (see "A Salish Journey through the Bitterroot Valley" in part 1 of this volume). During the negotiations, the Salish were led by Chief Victor (X̣ʷeɫx̣ɫcín, Many Horses). The head chief of the Pend d'Oreille was Chief Alexander (Tmɫx̣ɫcín, No Horses). One band of Kootenai people was also present at the council; they were led by Chief Michelle.

From the start, the Hellgate Treaty negotiations were plagued by serious translation problems. A Jesuit observer, Father Adrian Hoecken, said that the translations were so poor that "not a tenth of what was said was understood by either side." But as in the meeting with Lewis and Clark, the pervasive cross-cultural miscommunication ran even deeper than problems of language and translation. Tribal people came to the meeting assuming they were going to formalize an already recognized friendship. Non-Indians came with the goal of making official their claims to native lands and resources. Indeed, Father Hoecken reported that tribal leaders showed "their hands unstained by blood," and asked, "'What is the sense of making peace? Have we ever been at war with the Whites?'"[4]

Over time, the real reason for the Hellgate treaty meetings became all too clear to Salish and Pend d'Oreille people. Under the terms spelled out in the written document, the tribes ceded to the United States more than twenty million acres of land and reserved from cession about 1.3 million acres, thus forming the Jocko or Flathead Indian Reservation. The tribes also reserved many rights, including the right to continue using the ceded lands for traditional purposes such as hunting, fishing, grazing, and gathering roots and berries. In addition, the United States promised to provide a number of educational, medical, and other services to the tribes.

Stevens was also intent on obtaining cession of the Bitterroot Valley from the Salish. Many non-Indians were already well aware of the valley's potential value for agriculture and its relatively temperate climate in winter. But to Stevens's apparent surprise, Chief Victor strongly resisted his demands that the Salish move north to what is now the Flathead Reservation. The Salish leader maintained the policy that had been the hallmark of Salish relations with non-Indians ever since the time of Chief Three Eagles and the encounter with the Lewis and Clark expedition: a steadfast pledge of friendship and nonviolence toward whites, and an equally committed refusal to accept unjust terms.

Unable to sway the Salish leader, Stevens ended up inserting into the treaty complicated (and doubtless poorly translated) language that defined the Bitterroot Valley south of Lolo Creek as a "conditional reservation" for the Salish. The valley was to remain a Salish reservation until it was "carefully surveyed and examined," on the basis of which the president would decide which area—the Bitterroot or the Jocko—was better suited to the "wants of the Flathead Tribe."

The Hellgate Treaty's confusing treatment of the Bitterroot Valley set in motion a long, bitter struggle between the Salish and the whites who coveted the valley's abundant resources. Chief Victor put his X mark on the white man's paper, convinced that the agreement would not require his people to leave their homeland. No other word came from the government for the next fifteen years, so the Salish assumed that they would indeed stay in the Bitterroot Valley forever. But after the 1864 gold rush in newly established Montana Territory, pressure upon the Salish intensified from both illegal non-Indian squatters and government officials.

In 1870, Chief Victor died, and he was succeeded as chief by his son, Chief Charlo (Sɫm̓x̣e Q̓oxʷqeys, Claw of the Little Grizzly). Like his father, Chief Charlo adhered to a policy of nonviolent resistance. He asserted both friendship with non-Indians and insistence on Salish rights—including the right to remain in the Bitterroot. But territorial citizens and officials thought the new chief could be pressured into capitulating. In 1871, they successfully lobbied President Ulysses S. Grant to declare that the survey required by the treaty had been conducted and that it had found that the Jocko (Flat-head) Reservation was better suited to the needs of the Salish. On the basis of Grant's executive order, Congress sent a delegation, led by future president James Garfield, to make arrangements with the tribe for their removal. Chief Charlo ignored their demands and even their threats of bloodshed, and he again refused to sign any agreement to leave. U. S. officials then simply forged Chief Charlo's X onto the official copy of the agreement that was sent to the Senate for ratification. The Salish still refused to be moved, and most tribal people remained in the Bitterroot with Chief Charlo.

In succeeding years, as pressures mounted, the Salish continued to walk the difficult path of both asserting our rights and avoiding conflict with non-Indians. This path was sorely tested in July 1877, when Chief Joseph and the nontreaty Nez Perce, pursued by the U.S. Army, moved east over Lolo Pass and approached the Bitterroot Valley. Some white settlers in Montana, the memory of Custer's defeat at the Little Bighorn the previous year fresh in their minds, frantically raised an alarm about a supposed Salish alliance with the Nez Perce to exterminate all whites in the region, who had minimal defenses. In actuality, Chief Charlo realized war with the whites would be disastrous, and he refused to ally with the Nez Perce—even though they were not only the ancient allies of the Salish, but also, in many cases, our close relations. Both the Salish and the Pend d'Oreille did, however, extend an offer to the Nez Perce to live peacefully among us and travel through our lands.[5] In effect, the Salish functioned as a buffer

Left: *Tzi-kal-tza, Nez Perce or Salish son of Clark, c. 1866.*

Above right: *Salish at Łqełmls̓ (Stevensville) during forced removal from Bitterroot Valley, 1891.*

between the opposing sides, enabling the Nez Perce to move peacefully through the Bitterroot Valley.

Chief Joseph's band moved on to the Big Hole Valley, where the U.S. Army attacked their sleeping camp and killed many people—mostly women and children—before Nez Perce warriors rallied and pinned the soldiers down. Eventually, Chief Joseph and most of his band surrendered to the army in the Bear's Paw Mountains in north-central Montana. Relatively few elders survived the four-month-long, twelve-hundred-mile flight from the army, but among those still alive at Chief Joseph's surrender was a man named Tzi-kal-tza. He was the son of William Clark. Along with the rest of the defeated band, Tzi-kal-tza, by then seventy-two years old, was

sent to a prison camp in Indian Territory (Oklahoma). And like so many other Nez Perce, he perished in the squalid, malaria-infested camp.[6]

It was not long after the Nez Perce war that the balance of power in western Montana was decisively changed by the construction of the Northern Pacific Railroad through the region, and through the Flathead Reservation itself, over the bitter objections of tribal leaders. The railroad's completion in 1883, and the simultaneous elimination of the great buffalo herds, marginalized the Indian way of life that had defined the region for thousands of years. It was the ultimate realization of the expedition's central purpose—the development of transcontinental commerce. And the consequence of the expansion of non-Indian power into the West, and into Salish-Pend d'Oreille territory, was the dispossession and death of the people who were already here. We have seen that the Nez Perce war resulted in the death of William Clark's native son, and that the Northern Pacific Railroad figured in the death of Clark's Salish grandson, Sacalee. Perhaps these deaths in some way manifested the tragic historical meaning of the Lewis and Clark expedition, and its aftermath, for Indian people.

Only a year before Sacalee Clark's death, the long struggle over the Bitterroot Valley had finally reached its bitter conclusion. Conditions had become intolerable for the Salish by the late 1880s, after the Missoula and Bitter Root Valley Railroad was constructed directly through the tribe's lands, with neither permission from the native owners nor payment to them. Chief Charlo finally signed an agreement to leave the Bitterroot Valley in November 1889. Inaction by Congress, however, delayed the removal for another two years, and according to some observers, the tribe's desperation reached a level of outright starvation before we were finally pushed north. In October 1891 a contingent of troops from Fort Missoula forced Chief Charlo and the Salish out of the Bitterroot and roughly marched our people some sixty miles to the Flathead Reservation.

On the reservation, the U.S. government again failed to honor its guarantees. This time, officials failed to provide promised housing, livestock, and agricultural tools and assistance, or even to replace the equipment and household items that the Salish had been told to leave behind in the Bitterroot Valley. Nevertheless, our ancestors gradually rebuilt a life for themselves on the Flathead Reservation, establishing a number of irrigated farms through collective effort. Officials solemnly assured the tribe that now, finally, we would be left in peace, to live as we wished.

That promise lasted less than five years. From 1895 to 1901, a new congressional commission tried to secure tribal relinquishment of reservation lands in Montana, including the entire western half of the Flathead Reservation. Chief Charlo and other tribal leaders bluntly rebuffed their efforts. "You all know that I won't sell a foot of land," Chief Charlo told the commission. "You had better hunt some people who want money more than we do."

The oddly named Crow, Flathead, etc. Commission was only the prelude to far more aggressive and disastrous Congressional action. In 1904, over the intense opposition of tribal members and the chiefs, Representative Joseph Dixon pushed through Congress the Flathead Allotment Act, which opened the Flathead Reservation to white settlement. The act directly violated the Hellgate Treaty, which pledged that the reservation would be set aside for "the exclusive use and benefit of said confederated tribes."

In April 1910, the Flathead Reservation was thrown open to white homesteaders. Almost overnight, non-Indians outnumbered tribal people within the reservation and assumed a dominating social and economic position. From then until the cancellation of the General Allotment Act in 1934, over 540,000 acres within

The sign on the building reads: THE MISSION VALLEY WELCOMES NEW SETTLERS ST. IGNATIUS, MONTANA.

the Flathead Reservation were transferred from Indian to white ownership. The elders today say that when their elders used to talk about this part of our history, they would use an expression in the Salish language—χeyɫ uɫ snsxʷnčmčmeɫxʷm—which means, roughly, to steal openly and brazenly, to rob someone in broad daylight.

For a time in the late nineteenth century, the reservation had become something of a refuge for the tribes. But after 1910, even within the reservation itself, Salish, Pend d'Oreille, and Kootenai people felt a profound loss of both the self-sufficiency and the freedom they had once enjoyed. As Pete Beaverhead said, "When the whiteman came, seems like we the Indians were gathered up. Seems as if we were corralled, brought into a place where we were to live. Many acres of our land was taken away from us. Today seems as if we are only staying in a house. We do not have any more land."[7]

In 1905, the year of the Lewis and Clark centennial, a popular postcard appeared in western Montana, bearing the image of Representative Dixon alongside Mary Clark, the great-granddaughter of William Clark, and Mary's husband. The postcard was captioned, "Me and Joe Dixon Opened the Flathead Reservation." The

Above left: *Non-Indian homesteaders flooding onto Flathead Reservation, April 1910.*

point was clear: There was a clear line running from Joseph Dixon back to Lewis and Clark, from the allotment act back to the famed expedition. And the Dixon postcard likens the aid that Salish people gave the expedition in 1805 to the supposed aid given by these tribal members (including Clark's great-granddaughter) to Dixon in 1905.

As we have seen, tribal elders also saw these separate events within a single interpretive framework, as but two chapters in a single story. But whereas Dixon and many of his peers presented this history as a story of "progress," Pete Beaverhead and Mitch Smallsalmon, at the beginning of this volume, told the story as one of invasion and deception. In both cases, U.S. officials made a display of seeming respect and friendship, while actually viewing our way of life and our sovereignty as little more than impediments to progress. And in both cases, officials misrepresented the hospitality and courtesy of Indian people as if it were approval for the taking of our lands and resources.

Left: *Mary Clark, the great-granddaughter of William Clark, and apparently the sister of Sacalee Clark;* right, *her husband; and* center, *Rep. Joseph Dixon, author of the 1904 bill that opened the Flathead Reservation to white settlement. Photo taken about 1905, used for a popular postcard captioned, "Me and Joe Dixon Opened the Flathead Reservation."*

The Survival *and* Renewal *of* Salish *and* Pend d'Oreille Culture

The Lewis and Clark expedition and the Flathead Allotment Act demarcate either end of a century of invasion of Salish lands and usurpation of resources—and also, a century of tribal survival against great odds. The allotment act finally came to an end with the passage of the Indian Reorganization Act in 1934, and since then, the formally reconstituted Confederated Salish and Kootenai Tribes have gradually been regaining control of the reservation and its physical resources. The tribal government has grown into one of the largest and most capable in the nation. In 2002, it employed over twelve-hundred people in programs such as the extensive Natural Resources Department and the Legal Department, which has won repeated victories for the tribes, including at the Supreme Court level. The tribes earn income from a major hydroelectric dam situated near the center of the reservation, and from timber production, the leasing of agricultural lands, and other business operations, including a resort hotel on Flathead Lake, where limited gambling operations began in 1997. Under provisions of the Indian Self-Determination Act, the tribes run a number of federally funded programs on the reservation, including Mission Valley Power, which supplies electricity to all area residents.

When limited resources have allowed, the tribal government has gradually repurchased reservation lands that were lost under the Flathead Allotment Act. From a low point in the 1930s, when the tribes owned less than 40 percent of the reservation, tribal control has climbed back up to more than 60 percent.

The reversal of cultural loss has been even more difficult than he reacquisition of the land base, but there have also been determined efforts in this area. In the late 1960s and early 1970s, a growing number of young people on the Flathead Reservation took a renewed interest in learning and perpetuating our traditional culture and languages. Tribal elders gave their generous help to whomever asked to be taught; Salish elder Agnes Vanderburg started a world-renowned cultural camp, which she operated each summer until her death fifteen years later. As we noted in the introduction to this book, the tribes established the Flathead (Salish-Pend d'Oreille) and Kootenai Culture Committees in 1974–75. These programs have grown into full-fledged departments of the tribal government. Our mission has been the preservation and revitalization of the traditional cultures and languages. We began systematically gathering oral histories and songs from tribal elders and developing cultural curricula for schools. The elders gave guidance and direction to this work, and after ten years they became constituted as an Elders Cultural Advisory Council, reviewing matters of importance to the tribe's sovereignty and cultural survival. In this role, the culture committees have also served to reintegrate traditional culture into the decision-making structure of tribal government, from which it was formally excluded in 1935 after the reconstitution of the tribes under the terms of the Indian Reorganization Act, which phased out the traditional chiefs.

During the 1980s, each of the culture committees established Cultural Resource Protection programs, designed to safeguard cultural sites on and off the reservation. In 1996, these programs were consolidated into a central Tribal Preservation Office.

The tribes have given special attention to the edu-

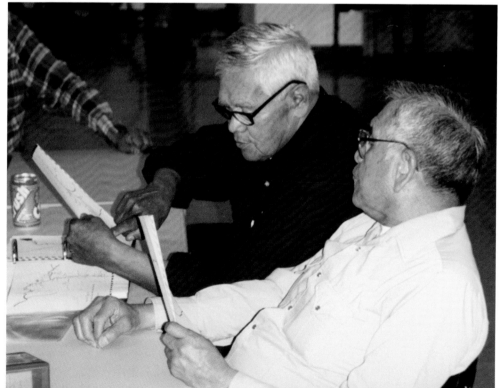

cation of our young people, and many educators have worked for years to integrate cultural instruction into the curricula at many grade levels. Tribal efforts were given a measure of support by Montana's new constitution, passed in 1972, which explicitly recognized the unique heritage of the American Indian and the responsibility of the public schools to ensure that it is taught to children. Many of the local public schools and Head Start programs have hired tribal teachers to conduct classes in tribal language and culture. The tribes also sponsor an Indian high school, the Two Eagle River School, dedicated to the teaching of tribal culture. The culture committees have developed numerous publications and other materials to assist in these educational initiatives. The effort to incorporate traditional knowledge into the educational system also extended to higher grade levels; Salish Kootenai College, one of the best tribal colleges in the nation, was established in the mid-1970s, with cultural education as one of its core missions. In 2002, the college had a student population of over eight-hundred. The Sqélixʷ-AqɫsmaKnik People's Center, a tribal museum and cultural learning center headed by former culture committee language specialist Lucy Vanderburg, also conducts Salish classes. And in 2002, language revival received a critically needed boost, as young tribal members launched a Salish language immersion school, where young people are being taught the language in an intensive environment.

Cultural revitalization is also reflected in the tribes' growing commitment to environmental protection. Due in part to the cultural leadership of the elders, the tribes became the first native nation in the United States to establish a Tribal Wilderness Area, protecting more than ninety-thousand acres of the Mission Mountains in 1982; since then thousands of additional acres have been given some form of protection to preserve cultural resources, wildlife habitat, water quality, and other assets. Among the protected areas is the Lower Flathead River corridor, where the council has twice rejected proposals to build more hydroelectric dams. The tribes have also set aside more than sixty-thousand acres as primitive areas reserved exclusively for tribal members and their families. The tribes are heavily involved in efforts to protect and restore a number of endangered and threatened species on the reservation, including grizzly bears, gray wolves, peregrine falcons, bull trout, and trumpeter swans.

Cultural and environmental awareness formed a key part of the tribes' response to a wide variety of issues in recent years, from the protection of air quality to the restoration of fisheries, from planning for growth and development on the reservation to logging in U.S. National Forests located in our aboriginal territories. During the 1990s, no issue loomed larger for the tribes than the Montana Department of Transportation's plan to expand U.S. Highway 93, the principal highway through the Flathead Reservation, into a four- and five-lane speedway. Because of the potential of the road to cause far-reaching environmental and cultural damage, the tribes opposed the plan, calling it the biggest threat to their well-being since the opening of the reservation in 1910. In 1997, the National Trust for Historic

Left: *Elders reviewing Salish-Pend d'Oreille Culture Committee draft publications.* Top: *Janie Wabaunsee and Felicite Sapiel McDonald.* Bottom: *Eneas Vanderburg and Noel Pichette.*

Preservation named the entire Flathead Reservation to its list of America's 11 Most Endangered Historic Places. In 2000, the tribes, the Montana Department of Transportation, and the Federal Highway Administration signed a Memorandum of Agreement to design and build a less destructive road.

For the Confederated Salish and Kootenai Tribes, then, the twentieth century was marked by a persistent effort to preserve and restore tribal sovereignty, traditional culture, and the environment so integral to our culture. Despite those determined efforts, there have been dramatic losses in all of these areas. By the 1990s, the number of completely fluent Salish or Kootenai speakers had declined to 1 to 3 percent of the tribal membership (somewhere between seventy and two-hundred people out of a tribal population of about seven-thousand).

Yet throughout this past century, tribal people have continued to follow the policy charted in the previous hundred years by Čełl Sq̓eẏmí (Chief Three Eagles), X̣ʷełx̣ìcín (Many Horses, or Chief Victor), Tmłx̣ìcín (No Horses, or Chief Alexander), and Słm̓x̣e Q̓oxʷqeys (Claw of the Little Grizzly, or Chief Charlo): even as we fought for our culture and our rights as a sovereign nation, we also maintained our pledge of friendship and nonviolence toward non-Indians. Indeed, in every major war of the twentieth century, for example, disproportionate numbers of tribal members served and died in the armed forces. Many of these veterans then returned to serve the tribal government in the continuing effort to defend and advance the cause of tribal sovereignty and cultural survival.

In the years that followed the Lewis and Clark Expedition, the world of the Salish was nearly obliterated. But it was not wiped out, partly because, throughout that time, the Salish, the Pend d'Oreille, and the Kootenai nations, and also a number non-Indians in the region, continued to work toward a relationship built on mutual respect and the honoring of solemn obligations. And so, despite the misunderstanding, the injustice, the loss and tragedy reflected in these pages, there is also hope to be taken from this history.

That hope depends on our continuing to work together to create a deeper understanding of our history. In 2002, the tribe was given a much louder voice when former culture committee director Johnny Arlee presented a theatrical pageant on the Salish and Pend d'Oreille encounter with the Lewis and Clark expedition. In several days of performances at the Arlee Celebration Grounds on the Flathead Reservation, some fifty tribal members gave audiences totaling more that four-thousand people a sense of the tribal cultural world that the expedition was entering in 1805, and the historical meaning of the encounter itself. The event proved that the bicentennial of the Lewis and Clark expedition can be about something other than blind celebration. The pageant performers, like the authors of this book, were motivated by a simple idea: that an unflinching reconsideration of that first encounter, and of the past two centuries, is essential if we are to reach for a different relationship—if the next 200 years are to been seen by our descendants as an era of greater respect, and of deeper understanding.

Clockwise from top left:

Johnny Arlee tells children the story of the Salish encounter with Lewis and Clark during the pageant at Arlee powwow grounds, September 2002.

Felicite Sapiel McDonald, Margaret Finley, and Michael Durglo Sr., July 2002, looking south from Kʷtíł P̓up̓m̓ (Ross's Hole) with Camp Creek valley in background.

Charlie Quequesah leads a line of singers during the Arlee pageant, September 2002.

Elders and Contributors:
Biographical Notes and Perspectives

This book would not have been possible were it not for all the elders who carried the knowledge down across the generations, and who generously shared these stories. In addition to the members of the Salish-Pend d'Oreille Elders Cultural Advisory Council (see p. xvi), the information in this volume comes from a number of tribal people. There is some variation in how confident we can be that the account we put on any given page is a true replication of that particular elder's voice. We have the highest degree of confidence in the authenticity of those stories that were recorded in the Salish language by the Salish-Pend d'Oreille Culture Committee. As we noted in the introduction, we have printed those accounts in a bilingual format to ensure that we are offering readers access to the actual words of the elders. Other elders' voices come to us in less reliable ways. Some spoke through translators, who then relayed the story to non-Indian researchers, who then wrote down their understanding, or their interpretation, of what the translator told them. Other elders spoke directly in English, but those accounts were usually written down rath-

er than recorded, and in most cases, they were written by outsiders.

Here we provide brief introductions to the elders whose stories, information, and critical review we have relied upon. Some of these profiles include excerpts of interviews we conducted with the elders about this project. We also provide mention some of the non-Indians who recorded elders telling stories specifically about the Salish encounter with Lewis and Clark. In general, all are listed in the approximate order of their contributions in this book.

Mitch Smallsalmon (1900–1981) grew up in the traditional way of life in the remote Camas Prairie area of the Flathead Reservation. Until his death, he served as the Wardance Chief at the annual Arlee Celebration, the tribe's largest traditional summer celebration. Like Pete Beaverhead (whose sister was Mitch's first wife), Mitch was a tireless storyteller with a vast command of tribal culture and history. He recorded dozens of tapes for the Salish-Pend d'Oreille Culture Committee archives, including stories, songs, and other information. The passages by Mitch in this book are excerpted from those recordings.

Pete Beaverhead (1891–1975) was one of the great Pend d'Oreille oral historians of his generation. He liked to tell of when he was a young boy, growing up in the area of Nṁłá Sewłkʷ (Crow Creek) on the Flathead Reservation, and the elders would gather to tell stories. They would send the children outside to play—but Pete would find some way to sneak back in and sit quietly and listen. And so Pete learned the stories and the knowledge, and when he himself became an elder, he was looked to by others as one of the cultural authorities of the tribe. Pete passed away less than a year after the Salish-Pend d'Oreille Culture Committee was established, but, fortunately, during those final months, he recorded scores of tapes on virtually every aspect of tribal history and culture. The accounts included in this volume are drawn from those tapes, recorded in the Salish language. They were translated and transcribed by culture committee staff members.

Alan "Chauncey" Beaverhead (b. 1961) is a great-grand-son of Pete Beaverhead, and, along with his brother, Gene, was raised by Pete and his wife Josephine. He is the youngest fluent speaker of the Salish language. Until 2003, Chauncey directed the Native American Graves Protection and Repatriation Act (NAGPRA) project for the Salish-Pend d'Oreille Culture Committee. His great-grandfather gave him the name Iłmxʷsqeẏmí (Chief

Eagle). Chauncey and his wife, Lisa, live on the old Beaverhead place at the base of the Mission Mountains.

Sam Resurrection (Nkʷílexʷncú—Pulling Oneself from the Ground) (1857–1941) was Bitterroot Salish, born near Łqełmlš (Stevensville). His parents were Baptiste Parte and Pleswé (Frances) Cuinche. His brother, Martin Kaltomee (1842–1919), was the husband of Mary Kaltomee (Sackwoman) (see profile).

At about the age of 9, Sam apparently died, but he came back to life during his wake. This was when he was given the name Nkʷílexʷncú, loosely translated as Resurrection. Thereafter, whenever someone died in the tribal community, Sam would attend the wake for its entire length, praying for those who had passed on and for their families.

After the government forced the Salish to move to the Flathead Reservation in 1891, Sam settled at Snłaʔpcnálqʷ (Coming to the Edge of the Forest, now called Schley) at the south end of the Jocko Valley. He lived there the rest of his life.

Sam Resurrection was a warrior and a leader, though not a chief. He was involved in virtually every major historical incident and cultural movement relating to the Salish people in the late nineteenth and early twentieth centuries. In 1877, he served as Head Indian Scout with the U.S. Army when Chief Joseph and the Nez Perce passed through western Montana.

The letter reprinted on pages 16–18 is a representative example from a long record of correspondence between Sam Resurrection and U.S. officials beginning

Left top: *Mitch Smallsalmon, c. 1935.*

Left center: *Pete Beaverhead at age nine, about 1908.*

Left bottom: *Alan "Chauncey" Beaverhead.*

Above right: *Sam Resurrection (Nkʷˌìlexʷncủ), c. 1915, at falls of Flathead River, drowned by 1930s construction of Kerr Dam. The dam was opposed by Resurrection and other traditionalists.*

in about 1907 and extending into the late 1930s. In these letters, Sam expressed tribal concerns, and tribal opposition, regarding a wide range of governmental policies, actions, and neglect. He helped lead opposition to the allotment act, the opening of the reservation, and the building of the Flathead Irrigation Project. He traveled numerous times to Washington DC, largely by hitchhiking and hopping trains. He protested for many years the lack of restitution made to tribal victims of the Swan Massacre of 1908, when a Montana game warden needlessly killed four members of a family hunting party in the Swan Valley.

Government officials often responded to Sam's letters with derision and dismissal. Such treatment did not deter him, and many elders today credit him with preparing the way for a number of tribal claims that were settled years after his death, resulting in millions of dollars for the tribes.

Many of Sam Resurrection's letters are an expression not only of one man's views, but also of the sentiment of the Salish traditional community as a whole. Sam was not literate, and so he had a number of younger tribal members help him write the letters, and he also had them read to him the government's responses. Many elders today recall Sam walking from home to home throughout the reservation, carrying papers in his vest pocket. Some of his letters contain many pages of concurring signatures or thumbprints of tribal members who signed on to his letters of resistance.

Pete Woodcock (1896–1978), was a prominent Salish-Pend d'Oreille elder from a family of cultural and spiritual leaders in the St. Ignatius community. The Woodcocks are directly descended from the great medicine man and prophet X̣alỉqs (Shining Shirt), who prophesied the coming of the Blackrobes. Pete himself was a prayer leader at wakes and religious gatherings. He was also a great storyteller and widely known for his infectious sense of humor. He was an original member of the Salish-Pend d'Oreille Elders Cultural Advisory Council.

Mose Chouteh (Čx̣awté) (1891–1987) was an important traditional spiritual leader and one of the most prominent Pend d'Oreille oral historians of the twentieth century. Known to most people as Blind Mose, he was highly respected for his vast knowledge of traditional stories. He often sat with people in his house at night and told stories until daylight. Like Mitch Smallsalmon and Pete Beaverhead, he contributed many recordings of songs and stories to the Salish-Pend d'Oreille Culture Committee archives.

Eneas "Tom Puss" Pierre (1908–1985) was the son of Bitterroot Jim Sapiel, one of the only Salish families to return to the Bitterroot Valley after the forced removal of the tribe in 1891. Eneas was the youngest of sixteen children, all born near Łq̓eɫmlš (Stevensville). Eneas lived there until about the age of six, when his parents finally moved to the Flathead Reservation. Despite his fa-

mously quiet voice, Eneas was one of the great sources of traditional Salish stories and oral history, and he recorded many tapes for the Salish-Pend d'Oreille Culture Committee. He was also well known for his humorous stories.

Pete Pierre (1900–1982) was one of the early elder consultants for the Salish-Pend d'Oreille Culture Committee. He was a particularly rigorous and careful cultural researcher. Pete held a particular interest in traditional Salish placenames, and he returned many times to the West Fork of the Bitterroot River in a relentless effort to track down and field-verify some of the placenames for that area.

John Peter Paul (1909–2001) was the war dance chief for the Arlee July Celebration or pow-wow, a cultural leader among the Pend d'Oreille and Salish people, and

Top: *John Peter Paul*

Bottom: *Michael Louis Durglo Sr.*

for many years, the anchor of the Salish-Pend d'Oreille Elders Cultural Advisory Council. He was an internationally renowned authority on the Salish language, working with tribal members and many linguists. He played a vital role in the Culture Committee's research into traditional placenames and tribal history. He was the last survivor of the Swan Massacre of 1908, wherein his father was killed by a crazed game warden, and his mother, six months pregnant with John, was forced to shoot the warden in self defense. John was raised by his mother, Clarice Paul, and his great-grandfather, Kʷtiⱡpú, in the Ronan area, where he later lived with his wife of over sixty years, Agnes Pokerjim Paul (see profile) and their seven children. John was known by the Salish names Šan Piyé (John Peter), Ċnpnó (Holds on Tight to the Enemy), and Skʷk̓ʷiml̓t Sněl̓é (Young Coyote).

Michael Louis Durglo Sr. (b. 1935) is a Pend d'Oreille elder, raised in the traditional way along the lower Flathead River, and an active member of the Salish-Pend d'Oreille Elders Cultural Advisory Council. He served in the U.S. Marine Corps during the Korean War. Until 2001 he was retired, having worked for over thirty years for the Bureau of Indian Affairs, primarily as a surveyor. He came out of retirement to work as a cartographer for the tribes' Indigenous Mapping Project, in which capacity he is painstakingly creating Salish-language maps of the entire aboriginal territory, including the spectacular map of the Bitterroot Valley area reproduced in "A Salish Journey through the Bitterroot Valley" on page 40 of this book. Mike had one child with his first wife, Lillian

Cox, and six children with his second wife, Barb Courville. Mike and Barb live north of St. Ignatius.

Reflecting on the Salish encounter with the Lewis and Clark expedition, Mike remarks, "At the time, I guess my ancestors didn't know the reason they were going through. And after you look back on it, to me, it's the beginning of the destruction of our land, or the way we lived. . . . Well, our young members, our Indian kids, they don't know the true story, you know. That's one of the reasons we wrote a book—our own point of view of how it was. So from there, maybe the non-members will learn how it was when Lewis and Clark first come through here—how we felt, and how we treated them. . . . when they first met them at the Ross's Hole, a nontribal member from this area guided them across Lolo Pass to go the Pacific, instead of our tribe doing it. That's how much we cared about it. See, if we thought it was a big deal to us, we would have sent the whole tribe over there with them, guide them, and went along with them. That's the way I see it. [chuckles] So when they first met him at the Ross's Hole, they just thought it was a group of people who were lost, I guess."

Mary Kizer (Čkʷutú) (1869–1955) was a Salish cultural leader and lifelong close friend of Sophie Moiese. Together they were leaders among Salish women and active in all major cultural activities. Mary was married to Michel Kizer, a traditional Salish cultural leader.

Agnes Pokerjim Paul (1910–2004) was a Salish elder raised in the Arlee area at the Pokerjim place, on the

Top: *Agnes Pokerjim Paul*

Bottom: *Duncan McDonald*

west side of the Jocko River. As a girl, she walked or rode horseback every day past the great larch that Coyote planted when he defeated the great swallowing monster. At the age of nineteen, she married John Peter Paul (see profile), who died in 2001 after seventy-one years of marriage. Together they raised seven children. For many years Agnes served on the Salish-Pend d'Oreille Elders Cultural Advisory Council.

Duncan McDonald (Tukn) (1849–1937) was a son of Angus McDonald, the Scottish fur trader, and his Pend d'Oreille wife, Catherine. He was born at the Hudson's Bay post, Fort Connah, in the Mission Valley. He was an authority on the early history of Montana Territory, a longtime member of the Society of Montana Pioneers, and an author of numerous articles for the periodical *New North-West*. Duncan was a longtime licensed Indian trader on the Flathead Reservation and served at numerous times as a translator. In later years, he spent his winters in Missoula, where he was a frequent speaker at the University of Montana and a close acquaintance of numerous professors.

Felicite Sapiel McDonald (b. 1922) is a Salish elder and the Senior Translator and Advisor for the Salish-Pend d'Oreille Culture Committee. She is called "Jim" after her paternal grandfather, "Bitterroot Jim" Sapiel (1856–1934), who was married to Ann Calasco (1847–1948, see photo, p. 62). Jim was raised in the Arlee area and grew up in the traditional way, gathering all the seasonal plants and going on hunting trips in the fall, when her family and others would pack over the mountains to the Seeley Lake area. She is a leader in all Salish cultural activities, from language camps to bitterroot ceremonies, from jump dances to powwows. Her beadwork and buckskin clothing are seen at every tribal cultural event. She married Louie McDonald in 1941, and together they raised twelve children. Jim helped guide all aspects of this book through to completion, and she is helping bring three other major culture committee books into publication. "I think young people might pick this up, and they might think, 'Wow! We didn't think it was like that!'," Jim says. "The way it is today, it's sad to me. We didn't live like that a long time ago. To me, I think the kids will be a little shocked. They wouldn't believe there was a life like that, that all the tribes lived that way. They'll learn something about their great-great ancestors. That's all I think about it. I'm glad we did it. It was a lot of work. We're lucky we still had some fluent speakers to help out with it. Ten years from now, there might not be any left. . . . I still don't go by Lewis and Clark. If it wasn't for the Indians helping them out, they probably wouldn't survive, or get to where they were going. That's the only thing I get mad about. They make a book about Lewis and Clark and they think they're the *ones*. Which it's not. Sure, some of them knew how to write about the trip. But the Indians knew how to travel and live. Our only written messages were the painted rocks. That's all I have to say."

Eneas Granjo (1883–1957) was a prominent traditional Salish leader in the mid-twentieth century. After the

Above: *Felicite Sapiel McDonald*

Bottom: *Eneas Granjo*

Top left: *Joe Cullooyah*

Top right: *Sophie Haynes*

reorganization of the Confederated Salish and Kootenai Tribes under terms of the Indian Reorganization Act in 1935, Granjo served on the governing council for most years until his death in 1957. He communicated often with Senator Mike Mansfield. He was a key source for researchers associated with the University of Montana in Missoula, particularly the anthropologist Carling Malouf; Granjo provided important information for the tribe's Court of Indian Claims cases in the 1950s. Granjo also enjoyed asserting and exercising the tribe's treaty-guaranteed hunting rights and was victorious in at least one major lawsuit on this issue. He led family hunting trips for many decades over the Mission Mountains into the Placid and Seeley Lake areas and into the Bob Marshall Wilderness.

Joe Cullooyah (1930–2003) was an elder from a traditional Salish family in the Arlee area. Joe grew up listening to the stories of the elders and going on the fall hunting trips around Čɫq̓lIʔé (the Placid Lake area). He served in the army during the Korean War. In his later years he taught Salish language to private students and helped with many cultural activities and presentations throughout western Montana. On many occasions, Joe generously shared his stories and knowledge with the culture committee.

Sophie Haynes (b. 1931) is a Salish elder from the Arlee area and an active member of the Salish-Pend d'Oreille Elders Cultural Advisory Council. She served as a Community Health Representative for Twenty-five years, and for many more years as a homemaker in the tribes' social services programs. Sophie's family is also part Kootenai, and she maintains strong ties to both communities on the Flathead Reservation. She and her husband, Dave, raised seven children. She lives just outside of Arlee. "I think it is important, the knowledge, what we've learned from this book—where they used to go, the trails, where they'd camp, and where they'd get their medicine, and their roots to save for the winter, and then for the hunting. . . . I think it's really important. And how they won't waste the parts of the animals, because they do use it, they use the fur . . . and then they use the hide. . . . And those bitterroot, and camas . . . that's really important for our kids to learn, how to save, respect our medicine, and our roots . . . and when they take it to the school, and that's when they learn, 'This is how our ancestors [did these things] . . . and they're trying to teach their own kids, so it'll be like the different generations . . . and our language is really important . . . our kids take it serious . . . with the

changes . . . pretty soon our kids won't communicate with another person to keep going. Then it'll die out. So it's important to keep it, too."

Louie Adams (b. 1933) was raised amid traditional Salish people in the Arlee area. He served for a number of years on the governing Tribal Council and today is a member of the Salish-Pend d'Oreille Elders Cultural Advisory Council. Louie heard the stories he relates from several elder Salish women. One was his *t̓upiyeʔ* (great-grandmother) Mary Kaltomee (Sackwoman) (see profile). Like his cousin Joe Vanderburg, Louie also heard stories from his step great-grandma, Sophie Moiese, and also from her close friend and relation Mary Kizer (see profiles of Moiese and Kizer.) Louie's account of the Salish meeting the Lewis and Clark expedition was recorded in English with the Salish-Pend d'Oreille Culture Committee. Louie served in the Navy for three years during the Korean War. He worked as a scaler and timber marker for BIA Forestry and Tribal Forestry for thirty-nine years. He and his first wife, Nadine, raised eight children.

Joe Vanderburg (b. 1937) is a Salish elder, raised in the Arlee area, who learned the old ways and oral traditions from his grandparents and also from his parents, Jerome and Agnes Vanderburg. Joe worked for many years as a professional graphic artist and printer for a number of printing companies and periodicals, first in Texas, and then, for most of his long career, in Missoula and on the Flathead Reservation. Like his cousin Louie Adams, Joe heard stories about Lewis and Clark from Sophie Moi-

ese (Č̓ɫx̌ʷm̓x̌ʷm̓šṅá), who was the second wife of Joe's *sx̌épeʔ* (paternal grandfather), Victor Vanderburg (see profiles). Joe's account was recorded in English by the Salish-Pend d'Oreille Culture Committee.

Victor Vanderburg (1868–1939), whose image graces the cover of this book, was a Salish leader born in the Bitterroot Valley. He related a number of his stories and cultural knowledge to the ethnographer Claude Schaeffer during the 1930s. His grandfather Grizzly Bear Tracks was a great Salish medicine man and warrior. His son Jerome Vanderburg and Jerome's wife Agnes were prominent cultural teachers for many decades. Victor was the second husband of Sophie Moiese (see profile). His grandsons Eneas and Joe Vanderburg also served as elder sources for this book.

Sophie Moiese (Č̓ɫx̌ʷm̓x̌ʷm̓šṅá, 1864–1960) was one of the great cultural elders of the Bitterroot Salish. She was appointed to be the leader of the annual bitterroot ceremony, and was known to everyone as an expert in many cultural areas, including berry harvesting and the use of traditional plants. She was one of the finest traditional meat cutters for preparing dried meat. She was the daughter of William and Madeline and the granddaughter of K̓ʷil Sn̓č̓l̓é (Red Coyote). Her first husband was Mark Big Star, with whom she had eight children, all of whom died young. After Big Star's death, she married Antoine Moiese (1851–1918), a subchief under Chief Charlo. Her third husband was Victor Vanderburg, the *sx̌épeʔ* (paternal grandfather) of Joe Vanderburg (see profiles). Like Pete Pichette, Sophie was also looked to

Top: *Louie Adams*

Bottom: *Joe Vanderburg gathering mountain tea at Lolo Pass.*

as a valuable authority by many non-Indian researchers, including Claude Schaeffer. The interview included in this volume is from a 1953 interview conducted by Ella Clark and originally published in *Indian Legends from the Northern Rockies*. Sophie spoke in Salish, and Louie Pierre served as translator and interpreter. Clark, however, did not record the interview, so we do not have Sophie's original words.

Ellen Bigsam (1880–1964) was one of the great Salish women leaders of the twentieth century. As a girl of eleven, she was among the Salish with Chief Charlo who were forcibly removed from the Bitterroot Valley to the Flathead Reservation in 1891. Along with Sophie Moiese and Mary Kizer (see profiles on pp. 132, 129), Ellen is remembered as čmaqs l esyaʔ—a person of the highest level of knowledge and wisdom in all areas. She was a leader in bitterroot and berry gathering, and a great storyteller. In one afternoon of work with a botanist from the university in Missoula, Ellen named

more than sixty different species of plants and their various uses for food or medicine. She provided other researchers with information on everything from traditional placenames to tribal history to the preparation of foods.

Clarence Woodcock (Čeɫl Spwá, 1945–1995) directed the Salish-Pend d'Oreille (then Flathead) Culture Committee from 1978 until shortly before his untimely death in 1995. He oversaw its development into an institution widely respected for its work in cultural preservation and education. Clarence possessed such advanced cultural knowledge in everything from language to ethnobotany to our spiritual ways that he was frequently looked to by much older people as an authority. A veteran of the army, Clarence attended the University of Montana and coauthored or edited numerous books and articles, including, with Robert Bigart, *In the Name of the Salish and Kootenai Nation: The 1855 Hellgate Treaty and the Origin of the Flathead Indian Reservation*. Clarence initiated the culture committee's Tribal History Project, of which this book is a part.

Pete Pichette (1877–1955), a renowned Salish oral historian, took it upon himself as a young man to become a student of oral history and the traditional stories. He was educated by his tribal elders and at the Montana School for the Deaf and Blind. Many elders remember seeing Pichette's large Braille books and Braille typewriter in his house near Arlee. He was looked to as an authority on tribal history and culture by both tribal members

Left: *Ellen Bigsam, Mary Ann Combs, Victor Vanderburg, and Sophie Moiese, 1910s.*

Above: *Clarence Woodcock (Čeɫl Spwá)*

and by numerous non-Indian researchers. He provided the anthropologist Claude Schaeffer with a great deal of information during his fieldwork on the Flathead Reservation in the 1930s. Smithsonian ethnohistorian John Ewer interviewed him in the 1940s, and researcher Ella Clark interviewed him in 1953. The passage in this volume is taken from Clark's interview, published in *Indian Legends from the Northern Rockies*. Clark apparently did not record the interview, so we must rely on her rendition of it. She mentions no interpreter. Pichette spoke both fluent Salish and excellent English, so he could have related his story to Clark without a translator.

Mary Kaltomee (Sackwoman, Smʔé) (ca. 1845–1957) was one of the great cultural leaders among Salish women. Her 112 years spanned a period of catastrophic change for the tribe. She was already a girl of ten at the time of the Hellgate Treaty, and she died at a time when communications satellites were being launched into orbit. She was the daughter of Shawnee Jack and a Blackfeet woman whose name is recorded as Mary Kalziishina. Throughout her long life, Sackwoman was a fixture for the people, a point of continuity during a time of transformation, a reliable presence at all tribal events. She was called Sackwoman because of her role as disciplinarian for tribal children. She would take disobedient kids, put them into a gunnysack, and dunk the sack into a cold stream. Oftentimes parents would only have to tell their children that if they didn't behave, Sackwoman would come. The kids would straighten up right away.

Sackwoman heard her stories of the Salish encounter with the expedition directly from people who were present at K̓ʷtiⱡ P̓upⱡm̓ in September 1805, and she passed her stories on to many others.

Chief Charlo (Sⱡm̓x̣e Q̓ʷox̣ʷqeys—Claw of the Little Grizzly) (1830–1910), served as head chief of the Salish from 1870 to 1910. He was appointed chief upon the death of his father, Chief Victor (X̣ʷeⱡx̣ⱡcín—Many Horses). Chief Victor signed the Hellgate Treaty in 1855. Chief Charlo, like Chief Victor before him, maintained a resolute policy of peace with the whites but also a determined refusal to cede control of the beloved homeland of the Salish, which was coveted by whites as the most promising agricultural land in the region. (See "Lewis and Clark in the Fold of Tribal History" in part 2 of this volume for an overview of the struggle over control of the Bitterroot Valley.)

Chief Charlo died on January 10, 1910, and he was thus spared the agony of seeing even the Flathead Reservation itself opened to white settlement, which happened just a few months later. Soon after, the government moved to evict Chief Charlo's widow, Isabel, from the chief's modest residence. The government said that the home was granted to Chief Charlo only for use during his lifetime.

Chief Charlo had three children from his marriage to Margaret (d. before 1888). They were Martin (1856–1941), Ann Felix (b. 1856), and Victor (b. 1864). Upon Chief Charlo's death in 1910, Martin was chosen to succeed him as head chief.

Top: *Pete Pichette in the 1940s.*

Bottom: *Mary Kaltomee (Sackwoman) in the 1950s, at about 110 years of age.*

Top: *Chief Charlo* (Słmx̣e
Q̓ox̣qeys)

Bottom: *Bud Barnaby*

The speech attributed to Chief Charlo, which we include on page 88, was published by the *Weekly Missoulian* on April 26, 1876. Chief Charlo made his remarks in response to an attempt by Missoula County authorities to levy taxes on the property of Salish people. We do not know who translated the speech or how accurate the printed text was, but years later, elders who had heard Chief Charlo's words as passed down through tribal oral tradition gave similar accounts of what the chief said; if not precisely verbatim, the text is accurate at least in expressing Chief Charlo's basic message.

Bud Barnaby (b. 1926) was born and raised in the Arlee Salish community and is an active member of the Salish-Pend d'Oreille Elders Cultural Advisory Council. He served in the 101st Airborne Division during World War II and worked in many capacities for the tribes over the years. Bud had seven children with first wife, Martha Curley, and seven with his second wife, Hazel Stanislaw. He relates a story about Sacajawea's grave told to him directly by Tony Charlo (see profile).

"Well, to me, Lewis and Clark's expedition . . . nobody ever wrote about our history . . . everywhere you look, there's books all over, Lewis and Clark, Lewis and Clark—everybody jumping on the bandwagon. So, to me, it's better that our people have a voice in there—our side. Because everything, even Indian books, people write about Indians . . . [but they] never really sit down with the Indian, and get the truth. I don't know when the Indians are going to tell them the truth, really. . . . And to me, like I say, it's better now that we'll get

something in there that the people can understand, and our future generations can read it. . . . But that's why I look at it—it's better for our younger people to be able to read some history book about Indians, instead of history about Columbus and all them. I think it's better for the whole society, really."

Tony Charlo (1905–1990) was a son of Martin Charlo (1856–1941), the grandson of Chief Charlo (Słmx̣e Q̓ox̣wqeys—Claw of the Little Grizzly), and the great-grandson of Chief Victor (X̣wełx̣ic̓in—Many Horses). When Chief Charlo died in 1910, Martin Charlo succeeded him. In 1935, when the tribes were reconstituted under the terms of the Indian Reorganization Act, an elected tribal council supplanted the traditional chiefs. Two of the chiefs, Martin Charlo and Koostahtah (the leader of the Elmo-Dayton Kootenai community), were allowed to serve as permanent nonvoting members of the tribal council, but when they died, the government did not formally recognized their successors. Many members of the tribal community, however, regarded Martin's son and Tony's brother, Paul Charlo (1879–1957), as the next Salish chief. And when Paul died, many people then recognized Tony as the traditional leader of the community.

Tony told the story of Sacajawea's grave firsthand to Bud Barnaby, who then related it directly to staff members of the Salish-Pend d'Oreille Culture Committee. Other elders have heard the same story related to them by *Snúwe* (Shoshone) people from the Wind River Reservation in Wyoming.

The account of **Francois Saxa** (c. 1820–1910) is one of the oldest we have, and one of the most detailed regarding the actual encounter with the Lewis and Clark expedition, but it comes to us third or fourth hand. In 1899, a writer and historian named O. D. Wheeler was compiling a centennial book on Lewis and Clark called *The Trail of Lewis and Clark, 1804–1904*. Wheeler asked his "friend Father D'Aste" if he could obtain the story of the Flathead (Salish) encounter of the expedition from an elder he'd heard about, "an old and reliable Indian, Francois." **Jerome D'Aste** was a Jesuit priest at the St. Ignatius Mission, and he wrote back to Wheeler on September 5, 1899. He had been told the story three days earlier by Francois Saxa, whom Father D'Aste described as having "the enviable reputation among the settlers of being a truthful man, on whose words they could depend." According to Father D'Aste, Saxa said he had been told about the Salish encounter with the Lewis and Clark expedition by "old Agnes, the wife of Chief Victor and stepmother of Charlot. . . . He said he remembered very well what the old Agnes related to the Indians about that historical meeting."

Saxa was the son of Big Ignace LaMoose, the Iroquois fur trapper who had settled among the Salish around 1819 and had helped lead delegations to St. Louis in search of "Blackrobes" in the 1830s. Francois and a brother accompanied their father on one of the last trips, and they ended up staying over the winter in St. Louis. Saxa's great-granddaughter, Louise Combs—who turned 104 years old in 2004—has related to us the story

of how the following year, Saxa's mother rode alone all the way from the Bitterroot Valley to St. Louis to bring her sons home, and then rode back, guided by the stars —certainly a journey of "undaunted courage."

When Louise was a little girl in the early twentieth century, some white people came to the Saxa home near Arlee, and as usual, Louise was told to run outside and play. But she pressed her ear against the wall, and to her astonishment, she heard her aged great-grandfather speaking to the white men in English. Saxa had learned English during his stay in St. Louis in the 1830s, but had never told Louise or other family members.

Father D'Aste was the first Jesuit priest to serve at St. Mary's Mission among the Bitterroot Salish when it was reestablished in 1868. He moved north to the Flathead Reservation in 1889, shortly before the Salish, under the leadership of Chief Charlo, were forced out of the Bitterroot Valley. Father D'Aste served as the St. Ignatius Mission superior from 1889 to 1891, overseeing construction of the still-present brick church. He also served as a mission priest from 1892 to 1896, in 1898, and in 1900. Father D'Aste served again as mission superior from 1901 to 1902, and then resumed duties as a mission priest from 1903 until his death on November 10, 1910.

Tribal oral historians usually maintained a high standard of fidelity in passing on oral traditions across generations, but the Agnes-Saxa-D'Aste-Wheeler account comes to us through several filters: the story passed first from Chief Victor's widow, Agnes, to Saxa; Saxa then told his story to Father D'Aste. Saxa spoke some Eng-

Top: *Tony Charlo*

Bottom: *Francois Saxa in 1859.*

Left: *Ursulines of Mother Amadeus's time: Boarding school Girls, St. Ignatius, 1886.*

Above: *Jerome D'Aste, S.J.*

lish, but we do not know if he told the story to Father D'Aste in English or Salish—and if he did tell it to D'Aste in Salish, we don't know who served as translator. By his own admission, Father D'Aste then waited three days to write down the story. He then sent it to Wheeler, who printed it—but only after making, as he said, an unspecified "change here and there." We have been unable to locate the original letter from Father D'Aste to Wheeler, and so we can't be sure if the changes Wheeler made were substantive or not. Nevertheless, there are many parts of this story that agree with accounts that have come to us more directly in both the oral tradition and the written record.

Jerome D'Aste was not the only missionary who relayed a version of the tribal stories of Lewis and Clark. In 1923, **Mother Angela Lincoln** published *Life of the Rev. Mother Amadeus of the Heart of Jesus: Foundress of the Ursuline Missions of Montana and Alaska*, a heroizing account of Amadeus's work. The story drawn from this book is a third-hand excerpt: Mother Lincoln's retelling of Mother Amadeus's retelling of what was told to her by an elder Salish woman known to the church as "Old Eugenie." We know nothing more about who Old Eugenie was, or what she may have actually said, or whether she told it to Amadeus in English or in Salish through a translator.

About 1908 or 1909, the photographer **Edward S. Curtis** interviewed Salish people about Lewis and Clark while gathering material for his multivolume work *The North American Indian*. In the published volume, Curtis does not say who among the Salish told him the story he recorded there, or who served as translator. He only states that it is "the native tradition of the meeting" with Lewis and Clark. In any case, the account generally accords with the stories told by other elders. Like so many of the elders' stories of the encounter, this one focuses on the misunderstanding and miscommunication between the two groups.

A passage told by an elder Salish woman named "**Ochanee**" (Ošaní, or Oshanee, the Salish pronunciation of the English name Virginia) comes to us through **Peter Ronan**, U.S. Indian agent on the Flathead Reservation from 1877 until his death in 1893. Oshanee told her story to an unnamed interpreter, who relayed it to Ronan, who then wrote down and published it in his 1890 book, *History of the Flathead Indians*. In introducing the story told by "Ochanee," Ronan wrote,

> At the date of this writing, May 1890, there still lives at St. Ignatius mission, on the Flathead reservation, an old Indian woman named Ochanee, who distinctly remembers, and relates in the Indian language the advent of those two great captains, with their followers, into the Flathead [Salish] camp in the Bitter Root valley, and the great astonishment it created among the Indians.

The explorers crossed over the Big Hole Mountains and arrived at the Flathead [Salish] camp in the Bitter Root valley in the year 1804 [sic]. Ochanee claims to have been about 13 years of age at that date. She is a lively old woman, and still has all of her mental faculties, and can describe camps, scenes and events which are vividly portrayed in the published reports of Lewis and Clark descriptive of the Flathead [Salish] and Nez Perce Indians, who were then hunting and camping together.

Above: *Agent Peter Ronan and family, Flathead Agency, Arlee, 1884.*

We are also deeply indebted to the contributions of other members of the Salish-Pend d'Oreille Elders Cultural Advisory Council, who worked with great care and attention over every line in this book. Elders not mentioned earlier are listed below in alphabetical order.

Francis Bigcrane (b. 1939) is a Pend d'Oreille elder raised as part of a large traditional family in the Perma and Camas Prairie area of the Flathead Reservation. Francis served in the air force. He remarks that "Lewis and Clark was the beginning of the downfall. . . . they came in, and then pretty soon the rest of the people started coming in. And then with the Sisters and Fathers, they wouldn't allow people to talk their own language. That's where we lost a lot of our language. . . . Out of six thousand of us today, maybe a handful can really talk it."

Clara Bourdon (b. 1937) is a Salish-Pend d'Oreille elder who was born and raised in St. Ignatius, where she still lives today. She and her husband, Leon, worked for seventeen years as the custodians for the St. Ignatius Community Center. They raised nine children together.

"I think this project is good for the younger generations," Clara says. "It's about time the people learn about the truth and what happened a long time ago. I think it's a good idea to publish this book. I think it's good for the younger generations, for them to read and find out what really happened way back then."

Alice Nenemay Camel (b. 1920) is a Pend d'Oreille elder raised along the lower Flathead River who now lives in the Ronan area. During World War II she worked as a welder in the Portland shipyards. She then returned to the Flathead Reservation and raised a large family. "Sacajawea led them across to Portland, Oregon and Seaside, Washington," Alice notes. "And she was the most important person on that trip besides Lewis and Clark. . . . She led them across all those . . . rivers—Missouri, and all those. . . . She even healed some of those guys that was pretty sick. She got sick on the way too. But they took care of her. . . . She was a very important woman." Alice notes that Lewis and Clark's encounter with the Salish was only a small part of the trip. "They only stayed a couple days. Even mentioned that Clark had a [grand]son by the name of Sacalee, but I don't believe it's true. . . . The third day, they led them to Nez Perces. . . . Seems like this book points out just the Séliš [pronounced *Sé-lish*, which has been anglicized as Salish] themselves. But they didn't stay long enough to lead them through the bad places, to the Nez Perce. . . . they stayed a couple days at the Séliš place, but they needed horses, and the Séliš gave them twenty, thirty horses to use. They even fed them, the Indian people fed them, fed them dry meat. They thought it was bark, or something. Tried to give them something to keep warm with, and then she put it over their shoulder."

Margaret Barnaby Matt Finley (1926–2005) was a Salish and Pend d'Oreille elder, raised in St. Ignatius and near Post Creek in the Mission Valley. She lived near the mission church in St. Ignatius. Margaret and her first husband, George Matt, had fourteen children together, twelve of whom survived.

Top: *Francis Bigcrane*

Bottom: *Clara Bourdon*

Margaret felt strongly about this project: "I think it's really great. And it's really neat for the children or anybody to read the book and understand all the struggles that we Indians took from the beginning—to come to the bigger reservation, how pitiful our people were. It's very sad. It made me real sad. But the . . . kids will benefit out of it. Somebody, even adults reading about it, will benefit out of it . . . if they read the whole book they would understand what Indians, how Indians struggled. That's what I think.

"I think it's nice, with the trails and [place]names, to keep it in sight, to keep the names on there. You go down to the Bitterroot or someplace, you see a little sign, it's got an Indian name on it, and it makes you feel good to know that people will see this name and they'll wonder why, and after you read the book, you'll understand why those signs are there. The name of the creek, the name of the trail. . . . A long time ago, it was no English, just Indian, and you go up in the mountains, and there's just a little trail, and it's called something, and a little creek just *barely* going, and that would still have an important little name. . . . It's important, when everything's got a name. That's what I think, about the trails.

"I think they'll get something out of it . . . some kids will read it, and then . . . they'll want someone else to tell them more about that. And an elder can tell them more about their feelings. I think they'll benefit out of it."

Octave Finley (b. 1928) is a Salish-Pend d'Oreille elder. A veteran of the Korean War, he served in the army and air force for twenty-one years. He raised six children and lives today in Pablo with his wife Edna. He is the acting Flathead war dance chief for the annual Fourth of July celebration at Arlee.

"The Ursulines didn't teach us too much about Lewis and Clark," Octave recalls. "It was mostly about Columbus. There was a lot of talk about Columbus . . . mostly Columbus, and the Fathers, that's what I heard about.

"A lot of us here, we're, like [a] jigsaw puzzle. We're piecing together . . . what each person knows, what each person has heard. We're just puzzling in the jigsaw puzzle and putting together what we have heard. That's about all I can say about that. We got to do what we can to make ends meet, to make people understand that it's hard for us.

"Everything . . . was taken. They was taking just about everything.

"Just like them . . . thinking that meat was bark, because there was nobody there to explain what it was . . . they didn't know what they was getting. They didn't know it was meat. They thought it was bark.

"It's been said their interpreters wasn't all that great. That's where we lost out on a lot of it."

Top: *Alice Nenemay Camel*

Above: *Margaret Finley*

Dolly Linsebigler (b. 1927) is a Salish elder raised in the traditional ways who worked for seventeen years as a translator for the Salish-Pend d'Oreille Culture Committee; she translated many of the oral history transcripts that are excerpted in this book. She was raised in St. Ignatius and still lives there with her husband Willie with whom she had five of her nine children.

Dolly offers her thoughts on this project in Salish:

Čn nte ńem x̣e ye q̇eẏmin ɫuqs wiʔičms ɫu t, ɫu t qe sx̌ʷsix̌ʷlt u t qe esyaʔ; qs mipnuʔunms l čeń u eċx̣ey es cx̌ʷuyi ɫu suya, suyapi. U čn nte ńem x̣e ye q̇eẏmin ɫuqs wiʔičms ɫu itox̣ʷ. U nexʷ ɫu t qe sx̌ʷsix̌ʷlt qs mipnuʔunms esyaʔ ɫu sck̇ʷul̇s ɫu qe ṗx̌ʷṗx̌ʷot ɫu qe x̣ʷlč̇mussń. U čnte x̌ʷʔit k̇ʷmiʔ mimipnuʔuys ɫu t qe sx̌ʷsix̌ʷlt ɫu qe nk̇ʷul̇mn ɫu esyaʔ. Tl̇ šeẏ m nexʷ mipnuʔuys ɫu t sx̌ʷsiʔix̌ʷlts ńe tix̌ʷ sx̌ʷsix̌ʷlt ɫu itox̣ʷ ɫu scx̌ʷlx̌ʷilts ɫu qe ṗx̌ʷṗx̌ʷot qe Seliš.

I think it will be good for all of our children to see this book and all of us to learn how it was that the white people came here.
I also think it will be good for them to see in this book the truth.
And then the children will learn all of the ways of our old people, our ancestors.
I hope our children will learn more about all of our ways. Then from that, our children's children, when they have children, they will learn the truth about the way the Salish lived, our old people.

Top: *Dolly Linsebigler*

Above: *Octave Finley*

Dolly continues in English, saying, "I believe that this book will be good, that people can read and understand what our people are all about, our Salish people. . . . I think it was about time that the people, the public knew what went on at the time [Lewis and Clark] went through here and met with the Salish-Pend d'Oreille people. And I think it's good that our children, our grandchildren, our great-grandchildren . . . start learning about their history, start learning what we're all about. . . . Our ancestors went through a lot to make this book possible. [It will be good] for them to learn the struggles that our people went through. And what it takes to have to survive in this world.

"Our people were strong people. They were gentle people. And they were . . . there to help. They had a lot of goodness in their hearts. And that shows in this book—the treatment that they gave Lewis and Clark when they met, making sure that they were fed, making sure that they were warm.

"I think this book will be a good thing for people who read this. They will understand a little more about our Salish people. There's so many things that the culture committee here is trying to put together, not only for our own people, but for the public, for them to understand what we're about. That we're not just a name.

"We have so much that sometimes our own tribe don't realize how much we have, how much that is so precious to us. . . . We have so much that we can give to our people, to our own children, grandchildren, great-grandchildren, we have so much to offer them. And what our elders would like to see, is for our young peo-

ple to take an interest in all the things that we do, all the culture traditions that we have. They should start learning and not be ashamed of what their culture or traditions are or who they are. . . . Like in this book, you can see how much struggle the people long ago went through. And it, they didn't give up, they didn't give up on anything. They kept right on going. And they survived.

Šey hoy [That's all.]"

Noel Pichette (b. 1931) is a nephew of Pete Pichette (see profile on pp. 133–34), and a former member of the governing Tribal Council. He served in the army in the Korean War. He and his wife, Babe, raised five children, and live in St. Ignatius.

"Like people say, they're going crazy over [Lewis and Clark] right now. Everybody has their own version of what happened at that time.

"It's for the future, what we put together, to make it a little clearer for our young people, or any young people that reads this story. And to understand the way we feel—I'm talking about us Indian people, how we feel about it, how we visualize it.

"And all these paintings that Sandoval made, I think we put a lot of effort in there, to try to get across to people how it looked back in those days. And I think those were doggone good paintings that Sandoval made. . . . What do they say? A picture is worth more than a thousand words.

"Way back then, our people didn't know what was happening. Most of the time, our people were so gen-

Noel Pichette

erous. And they were not selfish. So they were willing to help. They would help anybody. If somebody was lost from a different tribe, they would help them. And I guess you could say they thought these people were probably lost too. So they helped them. . . . They gave them horses. And Lewis and Clark and the company gave them a few little trinkets there, and they thought they were paying them. But I don't think they were accepting that as payment. It was just an exchange of gifts.

"When I look back on it and think about all the hardships those people went through, making their way—'course, they had an ulterior motive for doing that. But they were, I don't know, you might say great people for doing something like that. . . . Of course, back then, I guess you'd say they were taking over the country, and this is how the people were doing it. There were many different ways that they were taking over the country. I guess, back then, whenever the United States government wanted more land, they would just make new laws, and . . . appropriate more land, or push their line a little further. A claim. Claiming more land. There were all sorts of ways that they did that.

"In later years, they used religious people, coming in. . . . Before that, when Columbus got back to Spain, the Pope declared some kind of a bull or whatever that law was that they passed, and gave Ferdinand and Isabel the right to claim any 'discovered land,' or whatever they called it. . . . So then, any other country that came, any other people from different countries that came over, they went and laid claim to the land, because the Pope,

I reckon, said it was all right. So they came and claimed our land—without talking to us.

"And we were not educated. We didn't know the way white people used their skills at using the written word and all the laws that they made. I guess the laws came from the Bible. And when you look right at it, the Bible didn't really mean nothing to them. If they lived by the Bible, the Ten Commandments . . . they would have said, "Oh, we can't kill the Indians. We can't steal. We can't covet." But they didn't pay no attention to their Bible. That's greed, I guess.

"And in later years, there were people in government. . . . They said, 'Let's make 'em selfish.' And they set out to do that, and they did it. Like today, I'm selfish! [laughs] I guess, money, like they say, it's the root of all evil. You get some money, you want more. You get power, you want more power. And that's what they made of us. Well, most of us, or some of us. I can't say all of our people are like that. But I am.

"In my lifetime, there were so many different confusing things that I was taught by the white people. So my life has been full of confusion. I learned to believe this, then I have to learn to believe in something else. And my own native culture was pushed aside for quite a while.

"I believe some of our people went to the different wars and they believed in the Bible, the Ten Commandments. And I believe some of them couldn't get over killing people. That hurt a lot of our people that came back from the war. They never did get over it. 'Thou shalt not kill.' But then, the church leaders said, you know, they said, 'Thou shalt not kill—except —' [laughs]. . . . Yeah. It's really confusing. 'Thou shalt not covet thy neighbor's goods.' Unless you think you should have it instead of them! [laughs]"

Pat Pierre (b. 1929) is a Pend d'Oreille elder and one of the principal spiritual leaders of the tribe. He has worked in countless jobs during his life, from logging to mill work to serving as elderly advocate for the tribes. Today he teaches at the new Salish language immersion school in Arlee in addition to serving as an elder representative on the tribes' water rights negotiating team. He and his wife Linda, live at Dog Lake, at the far western edge of the Flathead Reservation.

Pat spoke in Salish of his thoughts regarding this project:

X̌ʷʔit ɬu tsq̓sip ɬu qe nk̓ʷul̓mn ɬu qe sqelixʷ čx̣ey es nɬpɬeptmm. . . . X̌ʷuy u čx̣ey, čx̣ey x̣ʷq̓ʷoʔscut ɬu šeẏ. Čx̣ey če ič tam u q̓ʷo es tax̣ʷllus ɬu qe nk̓ʷul̓mn.

Many of the ways of our people of long ago, it is like they are being forgotten. . . . Those ways have, like, like separated from us as time went on. It is like our ways is going the wrong way.

Tam qe esyaʔ u l še u qe ečx̣ey. Puti x̣ʷa qe čk̓ʷink̓ʷnš ɬu puti qe es ččnčnim ɬu, ɬu unexʷ qe nk̓ʷul̓mn ɬu qe sqelixʷ. . . . Ṅem tl̓ šeẏ m eɬ yoyootwil̓š ɬu qe nk̓ʷul̓mn.

Not all of us are like that. There are still some of us who still hold on to the real ways of the people. . . . That is how our culture will become strong again.

Łu tsq̓sip ɬu qe cčiciɬt ɬu tl̓ nisq̓ʷo ɬu t suyapi u tl̓ šeẏ u čx̣ey ctix̣ʷllm. Qe cqeyx̣ʷɬlt u ye lʔe. Ye l qe šnulexʷ lʔe u qe qe x̣̓lip. Če tam k̓ʷtnulexʷ ye qe st̓ulixʷ. U ɬu tsq̓sip ɬu putuʔ t še u cniʔek̓ʷ ɬu suyapi; esyaʔ ɬiʔe u qe st̓ulixʷ; tl̓ čsunkʷ u č̓ čsunkʷ. Tl̓ x̣̓aq̓lexʷ u č̓ ċaɬtulexʷ. Esyaʔ u sqlixʷulexʷ.

A long time ago, when we were met by the white people, from there on, our culture changed. We were chased until we came here. Here, in this area, is where we stopped. Our land is no longer big. A long time ago, when the white people came across the water; all of this land was ours; from island to island; from the south to the north.
It was all Indian land.

Ḱemt esyaʔ u qe es yoʔstem ɫu qeqs sck̓ʷuɫ.
Ta qe es qʷn̓mscut ɫu t sʔiɫn. Ta qe es
qʷn̓mscut t stem̓. Šimi qeqs čtem̓tn esyaʔ u
qe es kʷestm. . . .

Esyaʔ ɫu qe, ɫu semimiʔ iše t suyapi iše
cmimiʔntes es cu t suyapi, es custm
"History". T qʔenple qe es custm "Sm̓imiʔ".
Esyaʔ ɫu scq̓eʔey̓ u itam.
X̣ʷˀl šey̓ yetɫx̣ʷa qe es k̓ʷul̓i, sk̓ʷɫq̓ey̓mini.
Sqelixʷ scuwewlš u es q̓ey̓q̓ey̓, sqelixʷ
sck̓ʷɫpaʔx̣s.
N̓em l še m ax̣ey m mipnuʔuys sic stulixʷ šimi
aʔacx̣eys ye q̓ey̓min.
Mipnuʔuys ɫu unexʷ sm̓imiʔ ɫu l še u ecx̣ey ɫu
tl̓ tsq̓sip u yetɫx̣ʷa.
N̓em mipnuʔuys k̓ʷeʔs
yoʔoqʷisti ci k̓ʷiλt itnm̓us
ɫu scq̓ey̓qeʔey̓s.
Yetɫx̣ʷa
ye l qe q̓ey̓min esyaʔ u itox̣ʷ ɫu es meyyeʔm.

U tlciʔ kʷn̓ew pɫiɫt ɫu q̓ey̓min k̓ʷu,
k̓ʷɫu qe esyaʔ qe q̓ey̓ntem.
Šey̓ kʷn̓ew ɫu isnk̓ʷɫp̓x̣ʷp̓x̣ʷot ɫu λe sqlqelixʷ
ɫu λe čx̣ʷect tl̓ clčɫʔupnspentč,
tq̓nčɫsʔupnspentč, sp̓lčɫʔupnspentč,
k̓ʷɫu iše meyyeʔm ɫu putiʔ snɫk̓ʷk̓ʷmiʔis ye
stulixʷ, kʷn̓ew q̓ʷamq̓ʷmt ɫu esyaʔ
u itox̣ʷ ɫu scmeyyeʔ ɫu x̣ʷˀl šey̓.

Then, we knew how to do all of our own
ways. We were not without food. We did
not go without anything. Whatever we
needed, we had it all. . . .

All of our stories were told; when the
white people came they called it
"History"; we call it "Sm̓imiʔ" (our news).
Everything they wrote is not right.
That is why now we are working, making
a book. The words of the people are
written in it; the people's thoughts.
This is how the people will learn about
our land, by reading this book.
They will learn the real history from a
long time ago to the present.
The people will learn that the books that
were written by others were lies; what
they wrote was not the truth. Now, in
our book, everything that is taught is
straight.

The book would be even thicker if
everything was written in it.
Then if my fellow elders older than fifty
years old,
sixty years old, seventy years old, if they
would tell what they remember about the
land, it would all be really nice, and it
would be the true stories about that.

Pat Pierre

X̣ʷ'l̓ šeẏ u qe es mimeyyeˀi t sqelixʷ—
tma yoyoot ɫu qe nuwewlštn.
Yoyoot u ep snˀeys.
Ta qes xʷeˀcin še qe ˀawˀawntm xʷˀit.
Ta qe es xʷeˀcin še ƛe miip
ɫu qe scntels.
X̣ʷ'l̓ šeẏ u yoyoot ɫu qe nuwewlštn.
X̣ʷ'l̓ šeẏ u yetɫxʷa qe es mimeyeˀm
ɫu qe sccm̓el̓t geɫ kʷnnuˀunms ɫu qe
nuwewlštn. . . .

X̣ʷ'l̓ šeẏ yetɫxʷa u iše qe, qe cuti, "K̓ʷmiˀ l čeṅ
u ec̓ẋey u t esyaˀ qe snkʷsqelixʷ
eɫ cp̓lču̓ˀusm, u eɫ kʷeˀeys ɫu qe nk̓ʷul̓mn. Eɫ
c̓nap ɫu l snihew̓sm.
X̣eyɫ kʷńew qʷu eɫ yoyoot.
K̓ʷńew qʷu eɫ yoˀpẏewt. Ta t stem̓ qeqs
mˀeč̓tmɫlt kʷɫu qe eɫ kʷnnuntm esyaˀ ɫu qe
nk̓ʷul̓mn."

Še ye iˀs meyyeˀm yetɫxʷa ye ye sm̓im̓iˀ,
tsńe cn cu "History",
itam. ƛe, ƛe čn cˀaċ̓l̓qeẏmi
u ac̓ˀac̓ẋn ɫu scq̓eẏs ɫu suyapi,
itam, tam une.
X̣ʷa snspsu x̣ʷa sck̓ʷɫpaˀx x̣ʷa stem̓ ɫu q̓eẏnteˀes. . . .

Ɫu t qˀenple ɫu qe sqelixʷ, ɫu qe ˀuwewlš
ɫu qe m̓im̓iˀim̓ ɫu putiˀ qe es mistem ɫu
tsq̓sip qe m̓iˀm̓ˀintem, seẏ ɫu itoẋ.
Šeẏ ɫu ṅem, ṅem ɫu ṅe čna es sunum̓t čna

That is why we are teaching our language—
because our language has strength. It is
strong and it has value. We do not say many
words, but much is said. We do not say
many words and already what we want to say
is known.
That is why our language has
strength. That is why at the present time
we are teaching our children to take back our
language. . . .

That is why now we say, "I hope
somehow all our fellow tribesmen will turn
around and take back our ways. It will be
put back in the middle we would become
strong again. We would be able to make
our living again. Nothing would bother
us if only we could take back all of our
ways."

Now this that I am telling about, this
news, a while ago I said "History", it is
not right. I was already in school when I
looked at the writing of the white people,
it was wrong. Maybe it was dreams or
maybe someone's thoughts that was written. . . .

When our people spoke told the stories
that we knew of long ago, the stories
were right. If someone listens to these
stories, when someone looks at this

aċxeys ye q̇eẏmin ṅem cu, "Šeẏ ɫu une".
X̣ʔl̓ šeẏ u yetɫx̣ʷa qe q̇ʷeyɫmiʔ qe es k̓ʷɫ
q̇eẏmini. Sqelixʷ sṁiṁiʔs, sqelixʷ scmeyyeʔs,
šeẏ ɫu qeqs tk̓ʷum. Šeẏ ɫu qes šʔiti. Ṅeqs
mipnuʔunms ye, ye t k̓ʷiʌ̓t; ye t suyapi, ɫu t
k̓ʷiʌ̓t qs mipnuʔunms. "ʔa, k̓ʷ l še u eċxey.
K̓ʷ šeẏ."

Es oyym ɫu sqelixʷ ɫu tsq̇si.
Ċx̣ey es k̓ʷupm, es k̓ʷplwism.
K̓ʷeṁt q̇eyiʔim t sṁiṁiʔ še č tam u es
tax̣ʷllus. Yetɫx̣ʷa qeɫ tx̣ʷmim.
K̓ʷmiʔ, k̓ʷmiʔ eɫ tx̣ʷox̣ʷ,
tx̣ʷmil̓š esyaʔ ɫu qe scmeyyeʔ ṅe qes miiʔims,
ṅe qs mipnuʔunms
k̓ʷi tam ci ci suyapi scq̇eẏs.
Č tam u es tax̣ʷllus.
Ɫu sqelixʷ es mistes putiʔ.

Ɫu q̓ʷoyʔe ɫu čn cṗx̣ʷtil̓š u čṅes sunuṁt es
ṁiṁištẇe. Es meyyeʔstm
ɫu šeẏ x̣ʷiċɫtn ɫu l isx̣ʷsix̣ʷlt.
Esyaʔ ɫu l islsileʔ, isxpx̣epeʔ,
iṗṫupiyeʔ. Esyaʔ ṅem x̣ʷiʔiċɫtn qs
yoʔnuʔunms esyaʔ ɫu qe nk̓ʷulmn ɫu
maliyemistn. . . .

Qe es tx̣ʷmim ɫu qe sṁiṁiʔ ɫu sqelixʷ
sṁiṁiʔs ɫu tl̓ tsq̇sip u yetɫx̣ʷa.
K̓ʷmiʔ, k̓ʷmiʔ esyaʔ ɫu uɫ ṗx̣ʷṗx̣ʷot
sqelixʷ k̓ʷmiʔ esyaʔ u ep sṁiṁiʔ meyyeʔs ɫu l

book; they will say, "That is the truth."
That is why now we are doing our best to
write this book. It is our peoples history,
our stories that we are going to put in
writing. That will be first. Then the white
people will learn. "Yes, that is how it was.
That is right."

The people of long ago were abused. It
is like they were being pushed around.
Then they would write history and it
would turn out wrong. At the present
time we will straighten it out. I hope, I
hope the stories will all get straightened
out, so that everyone will know that the
white people's writing is wrong. They are
going in the wrong direction.
The people still know the stories.

Myself, when I was growing up I listened
to the story telling. What was told to me
I will give to my children. All of it to
my daughters' children, my sons' children,
my great-grandchildren. I will give it all
to them so they may learn all of our
ways, our medicines. . . .

We are straightening the history, the
people's history from a long time ago to
the present. I hope that all of our elders
of our people would tell their history and

še u ečx̣ey łu unex̌ʷ l se u ečx̣ey. Yetłx̣ʷa
qe es q̓ʷeyłmiɂsti
ye x̣ʷl q̓eymin
ṅe qs mipnuɂunms łu i tox̣ʷ; putu lše u ečx̣ey.
Tam łu suyapi sṁiṁiɂs. . . .

Še yetłwa lemlmtš
u čṅep scuwewlš. K̓ʷmiɂ, kʷmiɂ sunuṁt łu
isnkʷsqelix̌ʷ łu l iscɂuwewlš.
Łu qe es lq̓laq̓isti iše
čn čučawm łu ṅe x̣est łu i šušẁeł, ṅe x̣est
nx̣saqs, isclq̓laq̓ist, isccučaw, in nk̓ʷulmn,
ṅem x̌ʷuy put čeṅ m čṅeł k̓ʷłɂaċxmist m
wičn—hayo! Cłp̓im łu isnkʷsqelix̌ʷ, es
ʔeɂems łu x̣est nx̣stin ye l sṫulix̌ʷ.
Nyoɂpy̓eẁtn qs x̣esti.
Šey̓ šey̓ łu isccučaw.

K̓ʷmiɂ l še u ečx̣ey.
K̓ʷmiɂ esyaɂ łu isnkʷsqelix̌ʷ u cplču̓ɂusm u eł
qllx̌ʷwiɂil̓š.

how it was, the real truth. At the present time, we are doing our best with this book, so that everyone will learn what is right, the truth.
Not the white people's history. . . .

So today, thank you that I have something to say. I hope, hope that my fellow tribesmen will listen to what I have said. When we went to sweat I have prayed that if my road is good, my sweats were good and my prayers and ways were good, someday I would look around and see—hayo! The people are lined up, doing the good things of this earth. We hope it will go in a real good way. That is my prayer.

I hope that it will be that way.
I hope all my fellow tribesmen will turn back to our ways.

Josephine Paul Quequesah

Josephine Paul Quequesah (b. 1937) is a daughter of John Peter Paul and Agnes Pokerjim Paul (see profiles on pp. 128–30), and she currently works as a translator for the Salish-Pend d'Oreille Culture Committee. She raised ten children—eight with her first husband, Eneas Inmee, and two with her second husband, Jim Hawk. Her third husband was Pete Quequesah. She lives in St. Ignatius.

Josephine sees a clear purpose in this project. "We're all trying to get the point across how our lives are. Be-cause we are different from the other people, from the white people, you might just as well say. . . . And I don't think of people as somebody lower or higher than oth-ers. Everybody's equal in my eyes. But there's times, in the years that I lived when I was young . . . of course, I was belittled when I went to school. I had the hard times with white people. But I think now it's getting to the point where a lot of people understand. It's good we're writing the book. We're bringing it out—how we lived,

Above: *Stephen Smallsalmon*

Right: *Oshanee Barnaby, Flathead Reservation, 1906.*

how everything turned out. And at least they'll have some understanding that we are who we are. . . . I think it's good. And now, since they have, the culture committee has this, the language and the culture, I think it's coming across to where these children are learning how to understand different things. I see it in my grandchildren. And I see it in different people, how they have more understanding . . . they're showing a little more respect for what we do. . . . Because ten, twenty years from now, you can imagine how everything's going to be. . . .

It's good you have it on paper. . . . That way, everybody will know. They can read about it. That's my feeling."

Stephen Smallsalmon (b. 1939) is a Pend d'Oreille elder and the son of Mitch Smallsalmon. He works as an actor in film and on stage, and he teaches Salish language in Head Start programs and at the *Nkʷusm* immersion school in Arlee. He and his wife, Juanita, live at the base of the Mission Mountains south of Ronan.

"The book that we finished, I liked it," says Stephen.

"It took many, many hours with the elders . . . sitting together, and talk about the book, about how should it be done, Lewis and Clark, and where the camping areas were. . . . And about the pictures, we changed some scenes, or rivers, or camping areas a little bit. And that was good, that was exciting to me—just sitting around and talking about it. . . . Because when you do these things, then you just imagine yourself in it. You can picture yourself right in the middle of it.

"This book is really something to me. I think it'll bring it out to the people. Because there are not very many books of ours, and our young generation should know about these. . . . The book, it's really wonderful from the start. . . . I hope people pick it up and read it. . . . It was great. It was just a great thing to me."

John Stanislaw (b. 1932) is a Pend d'Oreille elder born near the Montana-Idaho border when his parents were camped there picking huckleberries. He was raised in the traditional ways at Camas Prairie, where he still lives today. For him, the book is all about the changes that have come to this land since the arrival of non-Indians:

Łu ƛ̓e es t̓x̌ʷt̓x̌ʷmulexʷ yetłx̌ʷa łiʔe. . . . — At this time the land has changed. . . .

K̓ʷem̓t šey̓ łu tsq̓si kʷm — So long ago, of course, there were

ta epł łp̓łp̓ulexʷtn łu tsq̓si. — not any land measurements done. All

L še u eċx̌ey es mlk̓ʷmulexʷ u ta epł — over the land, there were not any lands

łp̓łp̓ulexʷtn. . . . — measured. . . .

Če čmi u epł q̓ʷłox̌ʷmi łu stmtem̓ łu — Now, there are fences around lands

tłp̓łp̓ulexʷtn yetłx̌ʷa. . . . — that have been measured out. . . .

K̓ʷem̓t ye x̌ʷa x̌ʷuʔuy — Something happened to the Indian

yecč̓ʔe łu ck̓ʷłči — lands when the white people arrived

łu suyapi. . . . — here. . . .

U kʷem̓t ye cxʷu-u-uy — Then in later years, when the white

yecč̓ʔe x̌ʷa łu ck̓ʷłči suyapi u kʷem̓t cuntm, — people arrived, the people were told,

"L še mkʷ lciʔ" u we tam — "This is where you will live," even

sqlixʷuʔulexʷs še — though it was not their aboriginal land

l še u qmintm. — where they were put.

These issues are central to this book. "I guess it would be what you would call educational, for future generations, so they will understand," John remarked. He then continued in Salish:

John Stanislaw

Iše x̣e łu ńe es q̇eẏq̇eẏ.	It is good when things are written down.
X̣ʷa ńem eł t qe sxʷsixʷlt, qe snkʷsqelixʷ. . . .	Maybe it will be our children, our people. . . .
Tl še m es mimiste∍es, yoste∍es łu x̣ʷlˊ qe nqʷlqʷeltn qe nuwewlštn. . . . Es čmiyeple∍ t šeẏ še ńem eł yoyoot łu qe sqlixʷscut.	From this they will know and learn about our language. . . . It is known that that our culture will become known again.
X̣ʷa ńem x̣ʷa c̣xey taqs nłeptmntm łu qe nqʷlqʷeltn łu qe cuut ec̣xey.	In that way it is possible that our language and culture will not be forgotten.
Łu tl čis cp̣ox̣ʷtilˊši u qʷu cuntm, "Ta qes nłeptmntxʷ łu an nnuwewlštn," łu t p̣ip̣x̣ʷot u qʷu cmeyełtm.	When I was growing up, I was told by my elders, "Do not forget your language."
Qʷu es cunm, "Ta qes nłeptmstxʷ, ta qes x̣ʷelsstxʷ łu an nqʷlqʷeltn u łu an nk̇ʷulˊmn."	I was told "Do not forget, do not let go of your language, or your culture."

It is John's hope that this book will help in this way.

Eneas Vanderburg (b. 1926) is a Salish elder, the grandson of Victor Vanderburg, son of Jerome and Agnes Vanderburg, and elder brother of Joe Vanderburg (see profile on p. 132). Born during a family hunting trip at Seeley Lake, he served in the army during World War II as a paratrooper in the 82nd Airborne Division. He lives today at Valley Creek, near Arlee.

Eneas states that "I'm honored to have been included in this book—that us old timers was in on it. . . . I learned a lot of stuff from the old timers. . . . when they [would] tell stories about the old timers back in the old country, when they met Lewis and Clark and all that. So what I know, I learnt from them, and I told what I know, just a little bit about it. . . . Whatever I learnt, I just heard from Grandpa, and Grandmother. . . . So I'm honored that I'm included in this history book of our tribe. And I'm glad that our tribe has got a history on this book. They'll learn about how the Indians lived back then, and whatever they did to bring us up this far. . . . This stuff will be here later on, when we're not working in here. When we hear something that we remember from years back, it's good to bring everything up, so people will know what's going on. . . . It's good to be on that history book."

Janie Hawk Wabaunsee (b. 1928) is a Pend d'Oreille elder who is descended from the tribal people who saved the buffalo from extinction by herding orphaned calves back to the Flathead Reservation in the 1870s. She raised three children from her first marriage to Gordon Williams and six children from her second marriage to Kendall Wabaunsee. She lives in St. Ignatius.

"For the kids," Janie says, "it would be good for them to read all about the past, the present, and the future and what went on during that time when the Salish met Lewis and Clark. And I think they would like to know what part the Indians had in this expedition and the places where they stayed and how they were treated by the Indians. . . . I think that's really good, to know what we did to help, and how we fed them and clothed them and all of that. So I think that would be for them to know that their people had something to do with that expedition. And the placenames. . . . They'll know that it was a place where they met the Indians.

"When you read [most of the books on Lewis and Clark], though, you don't hear much of the Indians, what part they had in their expedition. So I think they'd be real interested to know what we did as Indian people all along the way to help, and everything else."

Finally, we make note of staff members of the Salish-Pend d'Oreille Culture Committee not mentioned earlier in this section. All have made vital contributions, at various stages, toward the completion of this book.

Antoine "Tony" Incashola (b. 1946) has served as director of the Salish-Pend d'Oreille Culture Committee since 1995. Before that, he served as assistant director, and in other capacities, since the establishment of the culture committee in 1975. As director, he oversees all culture committee operations, from the production of books to language work, from archiving oral histo-

Top: *Eneas Vanderburg*

Above: *Janie Hawk Wabaunsee*

ries, photos, and songs to the holding of ceremonial events and wakes in the tribal longhouse. He speaks on the tribe's behalf at numerous public events throughout Montana and the nation, and served as the first Native American to open a session of Congress with a prayer. He is a veteran of the Vietnam War and a former representative on the tribal council. A fluent speaker, Tony is the nephew of Pete Beaverhead (see profile), and was raised in part by his grandparents, Polassie Incashola and Agnes Woodcock Incashola. Tony and his wife, Denise, raised four of their own children and many others, including foster children, at their home in St. Ignatius.

Tony explains how for tribal people, the Lewis and Clark bicentennial presents a mixed bag of challenges, difficulties, and opportunities: "When this bicentennial of Lewis and Clark first started, with the people writing the history of Lewis and Clark, and Lewis and Clark's dog, and Lewis and Clark's campsite—you know, everything, I think I had the same feeling as a lot of the elders at that time: that . . . for the white people, I guess it *was* a celebration. And as we got requests, as the elders got requests for more information about the tribal perspective of the meeting of Lewis and Clark, I think I felt the same way as a lot of the elders at the time, that we did not want to get involved in any of this. We didn't want to be a part of it—mainly because we didn't want to feel that we were part of a celebration that in reality was part of the destruction of the way of life of the Salish and the Pend d'Oreille people, and all tribes, for that matter, in what is now the United States. The homelands, the lifestyles, the way of life—everything start-

ed to change [after] Lewis and Clark . . . went through here. . . . What Lewis and Clark meant, and . . . what they accomplished was, I guess, the beginning of the end for a lot of the tribes in this continent.

"So, at the beginning, like I said, I felt like a lot of the elders—that we didn't want anything to do with it. We didn't want to be a part of it in any way. But as time went on, other people more or less convinced me that this was probably a good opportunity to correct the history that is out there on the Salish-Pend d'Oreille people—the history that was written by other people, by nonmembers, by other historians, by white historians, by people who did not really understand or did not know the lifestyle of the Salish-Pend d'Oreille people. And I was convinced that this was an opportunity for the Salish people to actually tell their own story, tell it the way it was, the stories that have been passed down from generation to generation, with people that really understood and really knew the truth about the feeling of what took place when Lewis and Clark first arrived here.

"I feel that a lot of the things that are happening today, a lot of the books that are being written, they're still missing the fact that Indian people have been in this North American continent for thousands of years. They've been here forever. And Lewis and Clark is just a small part of it. . . . It amazes me that people don't realize they're trying to make something big out of an event that took a small part of the lives of the Indian people here. That event more or less just went by as far as the Salish people are concerned. But the effect of it, I guess, was really lasting. Like I said, we're suffering today because of that.

"So in a sense I guess we have an opportunity to try to do damage control, as usual. [In contrast to] all the books and information that are being written by non-Indian people, we as a tribe, as Salish-Pend d'Oreille people, can tell the story, the real truth, the real story of the encounter of the Salish-Pend d'Oreille people with Lewis and Clark—how it happened, what took place, the feelings that were there, those stories that only the Salish people can tell. . . . Those stories that were passed down from generation to generation, that we have learned from interviewing our elders over the years. So in a sense, I'm hoping that this will help clari-

fy or educate those people, strengthen our stand as Salish people, of the truth of who we are, our values that we're trying to hold on to. And hopefully that the non-Indian people will understand why we are reluctant to celebrate, why we are reluctant to share information in fear that it will be misinterpreted and misused. So by the Salish people telling their own stories, it will be their own words, it will be their own stories, so that it can't be misinterpreted. . . . So I'm hoping that will be the outcome of this."

Tony concludes with a statement in the Salish language:

Łu x̣ʷĺ in x̣ʷlčmussn
x̣ʷĺ šeẏ učn̓es q̓ʷeylmiʔ yetłx̣ʷa.
X̣ʷĺ šeẏ u qe es k̓ʷul̓m
łu qe sck̓ʷul̓ yetłx̣ʷa, x̣ʷĺ qe sx̣ʷsix̣ʷlt.
X̣ʷĺ qe x̣ʷlčmussn łu nk̓ʷuʔul̓mis.
X̣ʷĺ šeẏ u qe es q̓ʷeylmiʔ yetłx̣ʷa.
X̣ʷĺ šeẏ u qe es nte:
k̓ʷmiʔ eł yoʔnuʔuys łu qe sx̣ʷsix̣ʷlt łu ʔune
nk̓ʷul̓mis łu qe x̣ʷlčmussn. N̓e eł k̓ʷeʔeys łu
nk̓ʷul̓mis n̓em x̣ʷuy m eł yoyotwil̓š esyaʔ łu
sqélix̣ʷ ye l st̓úlix̣ʷ.

It's for my ancestors,
that is why I'm trying hard at this present
time. That is why we are doing the work that
we do now. It's not for me, it's not for us,
it's for, for our children, for our ancestors'
ways. That is why we are working hard
today. That is what we think: I hope our
children will re-learn the real ways of our
ancestors. If the children will take back
those ways, everyone will go and get strong
again on this land.

Shirley Trahan (b. 1944) is the Salish language specialist for the Salish-Pend d'Oreille Culture Committee, responsible for the overall Salish language effort. She is the sister of Dolly Linsebigler, who worked in the past for the culture committee and translated many tapes from Salish to English. As part of the work on this book and several others now in production, Shirley has created a number of bilingual transcripts of recorded interviews with tribal elders. Shirley accomplished this work, essential to our goal of giving readers access to the direct words of the elders, by going back to the original oral history tapes and transcribing them into written Salish. Shirley also wrote the "Brief Guide to Written Salish and the International Phonetic Alphabet" included at the end of this volume. Shirley was born and raised in St. Ignatius, where she also raised six children and still lives today.

Shirley traces her thoughts about this project back to her years as a student in the St. Ignatius public schools. "When I was in school and hearing about Lewis and Clark and their Louisiana Purchase, I remember clearly that my one thought was . . . was it really their land to buy, or for anyone to sell? And now, working for the culture committee, and listening to the tapes and what was said, really brings home that it really wasn't the French's place to sell all of this land. And it wasn't the right of the government here to buy it. It wasn't theirs. They didn't have no feelings, or no concerns towards the people who already inhabited this land. It was just like it was just a rug pulled out from under us. And I can imagine how our people felt when they heard about this and realized what had happened. And I really feel that was a very dishonorable thing, a disrespectful thing to do to the Indian people, the native people of this continent or this . . . land here. And I just think they did not give any thought to how the Salish-Pend d'Oreille lived. They didn't care. They just wanted that, and they took it.

"When I listen to the tapes and realize how the life of the native people was, I get such a feeling of, maybe not so much pride, but a good feeling—that we were a good people, that we had our own civilization. And we made due with everything that was provided to us on earth—the medicines, all the food stuffs. Maybe we had to work hard to get it, but it was appreciated, and nothing was wasted.

"After the European contact, I guess I'd say, our lives began to change from way back then. Sure, maybe they had things that was easier, made your lives a little easier, but now, a lot of that stuff that's easier was not good for you. So, you go from having a pure earth, pure food, pure air, pure water to so much contamination that's bad for health. . . . And the mental anguish, also that all of that causes is really bad. . . . People nowadays . . . think of themselves as dumb Indians, because they're not the ones who put all this stuff that we have now. But Indian people are not dumb. They're not stupid. If they could just use their minds a little bit, they'd know. And seek out their abilities, they'd know that they aren't that. That would go a long ways to having a healthy, happy nation again, in spite of all the contamination. Maybe in some ways we could reclaim our dignity and integrity and all the good stuff that we need, that our children need.

Shirley Trahan digging camas at Lolo Pass, 2002.

"I think this project is a good project because it will open some eyes. Maybe it'll open the eyes of the native peoples, and open the eyes of some of the nonnatives. A lot them already, I think they understand what has happened. And I think it's a good thing to do this, to learn this book."

Sadie Peone (b. 1982), a granddaughter of Dolly Linsebigler (see profile), is the culture committee's historical collections manager. She oversees the care and organization of the committee's extensive audio, video, and photographic collections, which include thousands of unique and irreplaceable items. She worked tirelessly in locating and preparing for publication dozens of the images used in this book. Sadie and D. J. Stops at Pretty Places live in St. Ignatius.

Gloria Whitworth (b. 1954) is the culture committee's office manager. She keeps the whole operation running, maintaining the books, helping with communications, helping organize meetings with elders, photocopying, helping in the kitchen when needed, and performing countless other tasks. Gloria raised four children and lives in St. Ignatius with her husband Gordon.

Richard Alexander (b. 1964) has worked for fifteen years as the culture committee's maintenance technician. He keeps the offices, kitchen, tribal Longhouse, storage areas, and grounds clean and in good working order. He prepares the Longhouse for all ceremonies, wakes, meetings, and other events. Richard lives in St. Ignatius with his wife, Bernie, and their two boys.

Thompson Smith (b. 1960) is the consultant in charge of the tribal history and ethnogeography projects, including the drafting of this and three forthcoming books from the Salish-Pend d'Oreille Culture Committee. He is also responsible for grant writing, ongoing work in oral history, and archival research. He lives in the Ninepipes area with his wife, Karin Stallard.

Corky Clairmont (b. 1947) heads the art department at Salish Kootenai College. An enrolled tribal member, he has been exhibited widely both nationally and internationally. **Tony Sandoval** (b. 1943), an enrolled Eastern Navajo, is a graduate of Institute of American Indian Arts (IAIA) in Santa Fe, and has illustrated many culture committee publications. His son, **Sam Sandoval** (b. 1973), an enrolled tribal member, attended IAIA and is the artist for the forthcoming *Beaver Steals Fire* (University of Nebraska Press, 2005).

Clockwise from top left: *Sadie Peone, Gloria Whitworth, Richard Alexander, Thompson Smith*

A Brief Guide to Written Salish

and the International Phonetic Alphabet

by Shirley Trahan, Salish-Pend d'Oreille Culture Committee language specialist

Introduction

The written Salish that appears in this book uses a form of the International Phonetic Alphabet (IPA), a writing system developed by linguistic anthropologists to represent all languages in the world. The form of IPA that we use has been refined for the Salish language through many years of careful work by tribal elders, culture committee staff members, and linguists.

Most sounds in Salish are also found in the English language and can be represented with English letters. A number of Salish sounds, however, are not found in English and cannot be represented using the English alphabet.

Here is the complete Salish alphabet:

A a   C c   Ċ ċ   Č č   Č̓ č̓   E e   H h   I i   K k   K̓ʷ k̓ʷ   K̓̓ʷ k̓̓ʷ   L l   L̓ l̓   Łł

M m   M̓ m̓   N n   N̓ n̓   O o   P p   P̓ p̓   Q q   Q̓ q̓   Qʷ qʷ   Q̓ʷ q̓ʷ

S s   Š š   T t   T̓ t̓   U u   W w   W̓ w̓   X̣ x̣   Xʷ xʷ   X̣ʷ x̣ʷ   Y y   Y̓ y̓   λ̓ λ̓   ʔ

As you may notice, Salish contains both unglottalized and glottalized versions of many sounds or letters. Glottalized sounds are pronounced "harder" or "longer" than unglottalized sounds. For instance, the Salish *p* is much the same as the English *p* in the word *people*. The glottalized Salish *p̓* sound is like the regular or unglottalized *p* but is made with an extra push of air—a slight pop. Similarly, the glottalized *m̓* is pronounced with more emphasis than a regular or unglottalized *m*. These differences may sound subtle to an English speaker, but they make for complete differences in meaning in Salish words. For example, the Salish word *pin̓*, which has a regular *p*, means "bent." But *p̓in̓*, with a glottalized *p̓*, is the root for the verb "to crowd." For this reason it is crucial that glottalizations and other phonetic aspects of the language be represented accurately in our written system.

Sounds in the Salish Language

The Vowels

a   the vowel sound in the English words *far, car,* and *are.*

e   the vowel sound in the English words *end, yes,* and *wed.* If there is an *e* at the end of a word, it must be pronounced. In Salish, every letter is always pronounced; there are no silent *e*'s in any of the words.

i   the vowel sound in the English words *see* and *week.*

o   a sound in between the vowel sounds in the English words *road* and *bought.*

u   the vowel sound in the English words *cool, moo,* and *boo.*

The Stops

c   a sound similar to the English *ts* sound at the end of the words *cats* and *rats*.

č   the soft *ch* sound in the English word *church*.

k   the *k* sound in the English word *key*.

kʷ   the *k* sound pronounced with the mouth rounded. It is similar to the start of the English word *quick* but is made slightly further forward in the mouth.

p   a sound like the English *p* in *paper* and *people*.

q   a sound similar to a *k* sound, but pronounced farther back in the mouth or throat.

qʷ   the *q* sound pronounced with the mouth rounded. It is similar to the start of the English word *queen* but is made slightly farther back in the mouth or throat.

t   the *t* sound in the English words *to, hot,* and *at*.

The Glottalized Stops

c̓   the *c* (*ts*) sound pronounced with glottalization (harder).

č̓   the *č* (*ch*) sound pronounced with glottalization.

k̓ʷ   the *kʷ* sound pronounced with glottalization.

ƛ̓   a clicking type of sound that combines the *t̓* and *l* sounds. This is called a lambda.

ṗ   the *p* sound pronounced with glottalization, producing a slight pop.

q̇   the *q* pronounced with glottalization.

q̇ʷ   the *q̇* pronounced with the mouth rounded.

ṫ   the *t* pronounced with glottalization, producing a slight pop.

The Fricatives

s   the *s* sound in the English words *say* and *yes*.

š   the *sh* sound in the English words *shut, push*, and *wish*.

h   the *h* sound in the English word *hot*.

ł   the sound made by pushing air along the sides of the mouth with the tongue behind the teeth. It is called a barred L or unvoiced L.

x̣   a friction-like sound produced in the same area of the mouth as the *q*. (To learn this sound, begin by producing a sound much like softly clearing the throat.)

x̣ʷ   an *x̣* sound made with the mouth rounded.

xʷ   the *wh* sound in the English word *whoosh* made with the mouth rounded.

The Resonants

l   a sound similar to the English *l*.

m   a sound like the English *m*.

n   a sound like the English *n*.

w   a sound like the English *w*.

y   a sound like the English *y*, as in the words *yes*, *pay*, and *yarn*.

The Glottalized Resonants

ỉ   the *l* sound pronounced with glottalization.

ṁ   the *m* sound pronounced with glottalization.

ṅ   the *n* sound pronounced with glottalization.

ẇ   the *w* sound pronounced with glottalization.

ẏ   the *y* sound pronounced with glottalization.

The Glottal Stop

ʔ   a sound made by simply closing and opening the vocal chords.
     It abruptly cuts off or starts a sound and is used before or after a vowel
     in some words. A glottal stop is similar to the break in the middle
     of the English expression "uh-uh" indicating no.

Long Vowels and Long Consonants

In words with double consonants, each consonant is pronounced separately.

In words with double vowels, each vowel is pronounced separately.
This pronunciation makes the vowel sound longer.

Archival Sources *and* Abbreviations

Allard — Doug Allard, private collection, St. Ignatius MT.

AMNH — American Museum of Natural History, New York. Claude Schaeffer papers.

APS — American Philosophical Society, Philadelphia PA. Papers of James Teit.

Beinecke — Coe Collection of Western Americana, Beinecke Rare Book Library, Yale University, New Haven CT.

Glenbow — Glenbow Institute, Calgary, Alberta. Claude Schaeffer collection, microfilm reels.

JOPA — Jesuit Oregon Province Archives, Gonzaga University, Spokane WA.

Malouf — Carling Malouf papers, at the Salish-Pend Oreille Culture Committee (see SPCC below).

MHS — Montana Historical Society Archives, Helena MT.

MPM — Milwaukee Public Museum, Milwaukee WI.

NA — National Archives, Washington DC.

NA BIA LR — NA documents from record group 75 (Bureau of Indian Affairs), letters received by the BIA, 1881–1907.

NA CCF — NA documents from record group 75, Central Classified Files, beginning in 1907.

NA-Denver — National Archives, Rocky Mountain Regional Federal Record Center, Denver CO. Primarily Flathead Agency records.

Penn — University of Pennsylvania, Philadelphia.

RCM	Ravalli County Museum, Hamilton MT.
SKC	D'Arcy McNickle Library, Salish Kootenai College, Pablo MT.
SPCC	Salish-Pend d'Oreille Culture Committee, Confederated Salish and Kootenai Tribes. Salish Longhouse, St. Ignatius MT. (Archives are not open to general public or nontribal researchers.)
SPCC OHA	SPCC Oral History Archives, including audio and videotaped interviews with tribal elders. Numbers following this abbreviation refer to tape number, the tape side, and the date. For example, "SPCC OHA 70/2 (1975)" refers to tape 70, side 2, recorded in 1975.
SPCC WI	SPCC written interviews with elders. Interviews that were written, but not recorded, by SPCC staff and/or consultants.
SEC	Swan Ecosystem Center / Upper Swan Valley Historical Society, Condon MT.
TPD	Tribal Preservation Department, Confederated Salish and Kootenai Tribes, Pablo MT. (Archives are not open to general public or nontribal researchers.)
UM	University of Montana Archives and Special Collections, Missoula.

Notes

Introduction

1. Minimal presence of expedition in Salish oral tradition—Joe Cullooyah, SPCC wi, 10-3-2000. In written sources, there is some indication that Salish and Pend d'Oreille people did sometimes relate stories of the encounter with Lewis and Clark, at least for the entertainment of non-Indian visitors. See, for example, John Owen, *The Journals and Letters of Major John Owen, 1850–1871*, ed. by Seymour Dunbar, and with notes to Owen's texts by Paul C. Phillips, 2 vols. (New York: Eberstadt, 1927), 42. In his journal entry for New Year's day, 1867, Owen reports, "Notwithstanding the severity of the Morning the Natives Made their usual time honored Calls giving all a hearty shake of the hand. The Old Chief Victor with hair Still Black as a coal—gave our Philada friends a Short recital of things that occured Some 70 odd years ago—Told them that he was quite a good sized Boy when those great Transcontinental Explorers—Lewis & Clarke passed here—which was in 1805." Similarly, Judge Frank H. Woody, a prominent Missoulian writing around 1876, recalled that "A number of years since, the writer was well acquainted with Moi[e]se, the second chief of the Flatheads, who was a boy at the time when Lewis and Clarke passed through the Bitter Root valley, and well remembered the event and many circumstances connected therewith, the party being the first white men ever seen by these Indians." Judge F. H. Woody, "A Sketch of the Early History of Western Montana," in *Contributions to the Historical Society of Montana*, vol. 2 (1896; repr. Boston MA: J. S. Canner and Company 1966), 89. Another brief reference was gathered in 1934 by the ethnographer Claude Schaeffer, who was told by Salish elder Baptiste Lumpry that Lumpry's mother said "that Lewis and Clark had the first mule that the Salish ever saw (?) The ears of a mule resembled those of a black-tailed deer. The Salish never cared for mules and seldom had any." AMNH Schaeffer papers, page 1–93. It is worth noting that the Salish do in fact use the same word, sťulčeʔ, to refer to both blacktail (or mule deer) does and domesticated mules.

2. While there is remarkable general consistency in the elders' accounts, there are also some minor specific differences. For example, Pete Pichette mentions a scout seeing seven whites approaching. Francois Saxa's account describes Chief Eagle himself doing the scouting, and seeing "about twenty men." For Pichette's account, see Ella E. Clark, *Indian Legends from the Northern Rockies*, 4th ed. (Norman: Oklahoma University Press, 1977), 143–45 (hereafter cited as Clark, *Indian Legends*); for Saxa's account, see Olin D. Wheeler, *The Trail of Lewis and Clark*, vol. 2, (New York and London: G. P. Putnam's Sons, 1904), 65–68, (hereafter cited as Wheeler, *Trail of Lewis and Clark*). The actual number in the expedition party was thirty-four adults, including Sacajawea and the African American slave, York. There could be several explanations for the discrepancy.

The party was moving in two or three small groups as they approached K̓ʷtiɫ P̓úpx̓m̓, so the numbers in the elders' stories could reflect that division. And it is also true that these two accounts, in particular, come to us not as accounts directly recorded in the Salish language by the Salish-Pend d'Oreille Culture Committee, but as writings from non-Indian researchers or historians, relayed to them through other people and interpreters. That kind of transmission can alter or garble many details. See notes on these sources in "Tribal Contributors and Sources."

3. See, for example, W. J. Hoffman, "Selish Myths," *Bulletin of the Essex Institute* 15 (1883): 23–40. Many of his stories can be found in later tellings. The story of Coyote eating birds while posing as a medicine man and kicking a duck in the rear end was also told by Eneas Pierre in 1975 (SPCC OHA 38/1). Two of the stories gathered by Hoffman—how lynx got his broad face, and Coyote learning he cannot be like other animals (elk, bear, and kingfisher), can be found in George Weisel's 1959 collection, *Ten Animal Myths of the Flathead Indians*, as told by Ellen Bigsam, interpreted by Joe Bigsam, Anthropology and Sociology Papers 18 (Missoula: Montana State University (now University of Montana), 1959). Hereafter cited as Weisel, *Ten Animal Myths*. Several of Hoffman's stories (e.g., how rabbit got his lip cut and Coyote gambling with the fishes), with some minor variations, were also collected by Louisa McDermott in "Ethnology and Folklore, Selish Proper" (master's thesis, University of California–Berkeley, 1904). Hereafter cited as McDermott (1904).

An even earlier collection of stories was relayed from the Jesuit missionary Gregory Mengarini to George Gibbs, who gathered ethnological information in the 1850s. See Ella E. Clark, "George Gibbs' Account of the Indian My-

thology in Oregon and Washington Territories" (*Oregon Historical Quarterly* 56 (December 1955): 293–325). Many parts of the Mengarini-Gibbs story of Amótqn and Coyote can also be found in numerous later works: McDermott (1904); in accounts told in the 1920s by Pend d'Oreille elders Lassaw Redhorn, Joseph Quequesah, and Domicie Michell to the writer Bon Whealdon, included in Clark, *Indian Legends*, 82–84; in W. H. McDonald, *Creation Tales from the Salish* (Billings: Montana Indian Publication Fund, 1973); and in Harriet Miller and Elizabeth Harrison, *Coyote Tales of the Montana Salish, from tales narrated by Pierre Pichette*, Exhibition of Indian Arts and Crafts Board, U.S. Department of the Interior (Rapid City SD: The Tipi Shop, 1974), 12–14. Hereafter cited as Pichette, *Coyote Tales*.

The story of Coyote as the sun and of Spq̓ní becoming the sun and the moon can be found in Gibbs (Clark 1955), McDermott (1904), W. H. McDonald (1973), and also in Pete Beaverhead, SPCC OHA 29/1 (1975), and John Peter Paul, SPCC WI (November 30, 1995).

Remarkable consistency over time can also be found in the story of the war of earth nation vs. sky nation, chickadee's ladder of arrows, and how animals came to be as they are, as told in McDermott (1904), Weisel (1959), and in Pete Pierre, SPCC OHA 25/2 (1975). It was also related about 1909 by Salish elder and translator Michel Revais to the Boasian ethnographer James Teit and published as "Pend d'Oreille Tales," *Memoirs of the American Folk-Lore Society* 11 (1917): 114–18.

The story of how chipmunk got his stripes is told in similar fashion in McDermott (1904), Christine Woodcock, SPCC OHA 1/1 (1975), and John Peter Paul, SPCC WI (November 30, 1995).

Part 1: The Salish World in 1805

The Mitch Smallsalmon quote is from SPCC OHA 171/1 (1978).

Coyote and the Ice Age

1. For the age of archaeological sites in western Montana, see, for example, Carling Malouf, "The Coniferous Forests and Their Uses in the Northern Rocky Mountains through 9,000 Years of Prehistory," in *Forests of the Northern Rocky Mountains: Proceedings of the 1968 Symposium*, ed. by Richard D. Taber, 271–90 (Missoula: University of Montana Foundation, 1969). Numerous Coyote stories relating to the events of the last Ice Age and Glacial Lake Missoula will be included in our forthcoming multivolume history of the Salish and Pend d'Oreille people. The scientific literature on Glacial Lake Missoula is substantial; a popular recent volume by a retired professor of geology at the University of Montana is David Alt, *Glacial Lake Missoula and Its Humongous Floods* (Missoula: Mountain Press, 2001).

The Big Picture

1. Congress passed the General Allotment Act or Dawes Severalty Act in 1887. This was an omnibus bill that established the basic process by which communal, tribally held lands on Indian reservations would be surveyed and then broken up into individual parcels "allotted" to individual members of tribes, with remaining lands declared "surplus" and opened to non-Indian homesteaders. After 1887, additional bills had to be passed for many of the reservations that Congress wanted to subject to the allotment, because the specific terms of the treaties by which those various reservations were established differed in significant ways. Thus, the Flathead Allotment Act was not passed until 1904—some seventeen years after passage of the General Allotment Act. For further discussion of allotment on the Flathead Reservation, see "Lewis and Clark in the Fold of Tribal History" in this volume.

"They hadn't seen our land yet, and they had already sold it": Pete Beaverhead, SPCC OHA 70/2 (1975).

"How can you claim land that is already occupied?": Chauncey Beaverhead, SPCC unpublished essay (1998).

"When he got off his ship he put his flag in the ground . . . just like he put a brand on this land": Mitch Smallsalmon, SPCC OHA 116/1 (1977).

"Three Eagle . . . order[ed that] these strange people were not to be mistreated or harmed": Sam Resurrection to Commissioner of Indian Affairs, NA, CCF-Flathead-131548-1913.

"This Land Was Good"

1. The accounts of the elders tell us that this huge dispersion was a westward movement, that Montana was the homeland of the original Salish Nation. Some anthropologists and linguists have argued that the Salish originated from the Pacific Coast and migrated inland. However, the elders are supported by other anthropologists and ethnographers, including James Teit, an associate of Franz Boas who conducted fieldwork among the Salish and Pend d'Oreille in the early twentieth century. Elders of other Salishan tribes told Teit, for example, that the Montana Salish spoke "the proper or purest dialect," and that they were "the head or parent tribe." APS Teit papers, no. 2446, no. 3207.

2. Steve Egesdal, PhD (Salishan linguist), personal communication, 2001.

3. Mitch Smallsalmon, SPCC OHA (1979).

4. Smith River: in Gary Moulton, ed., *The Journals of the Lewis and Clark Expedition, Volume 9: The Journals of John Ordway, May 14, 1804–September 23, 1806, and Charles Floyd, May 14–August 18, 1804,* (Lincoln: University of Nebraska Press, 1996), 184 (hereafter cited as Moulton 9); Three Forks: in Gary Moulton, ed., *The Journals of the Lewis and Clark Expedition, Volume 10: The Journal of Patrick Gass, May 14, 1804–September 23, 1806* (Lincoln: University of Nebraska Press, 1996), 118 (hereafter cited as Moulton 10); Clark's Fork near Missoula: in Gary Moulton, ed., *The Journals of the Lewis and Clark Expedition, Volume 8: June 10–September 26, 1806* (Lincoln: University of Nebraska Press, 1993), 86 (hereafter cited as Moulton 8); Blackfoot River: Moulton 8, 89, and Moulton 10, 249-50; currants: Moulton 10, 115; Bitterroot Valley: Moulton 8, 161 and 74-79.

5. Pete Woodcock, SPCC OHA 16/1 (1975).

6. Pete Beaverhead, SPCC OHA 49/1 (1975).

7. Pete Woodcock, SPCC OHA 9/1 (1975).

8. The story of the Big Draw is yet another case of the Coyote stories reflecting how long the people have been here, in that they tell the story of the same places that geologists now say were key sites in the geology of the last Ice Age. Glacial Lake Missoula backed up exactly to the hill where Coyote stopped digging his river to Flathead Lake. The hill was formed as a terminal moraine of one of the lobes of ice pushing from the north. When the lake drained, the moraine blocked the water from moving through the Big Draw and perhaps creating a route for salmon into Flathead Lake; instead, it drained along the present course of the Flathead River. John Peter Paul, SPCC OHA video (2000), and Alt, Glacial Lake Missoula.

9. Mose Chouteh, SPCC OHA 30/2 (1975).

10. The Lewis and Clark journals make repeated note of Salish fish weirs just west of Lolo Pass—the first place west of the pass where we could efficiently harvest salmon. See, for example, Gary Moulton, ed., *The Journals of the Lewis and Clark Expedition, Volume 5: July 28–November 1, 1805* (Lincoln: University of Nebraska Press, 1988), 204-5. Hereafter cited as Moulton 5.

A Salish Journey through the Bitterroot Valley

1. Pete Beaverhead, SPCC OHA 18/2 (1975).

Sources on placename Snⱡp̓up̓x̣ʷm̓: SPCC OHA video: SPCC and elders trip to Butte (May 1997). SPCC OHA audio tapes: Pete Woodcock and Agnes Vanderburg, 1/2 (1975); Eneas Pierre, 14/2 (1975); Pete Pierre, 15/1 (1975); Pete Beaverhead, 18/2 (1975); Pete Beaverhead, 42/1 (1975); Pete Beaverhead, 47/1 (1975); Mary Finley, 60/1 (1975); Mitch Smallsalmon, 157/2 (1978); Pete Pierre, 260/2 (1981). SPCC wi: Steve Egesdal working with John Peter Paul and other elders, December 6, 1998; John Peter Paul and Louie Adams, April 21, 1997; SPCC elders meeting, September 27, 1996; Mike Durglo, Sr., March 21, 2001 and July 15, 1999. Other sources: Agnes Vanderburg, Ignace Pierre, Jerome Lumpry, and Adele Adams, *Tales from the Bitterroot Valley, and Other Salish Folk Stories,* as told to Kathryn Law, interpreted by Agnes Vanderburg (Billings: Montana Indian Publications, 1971); Pichette, *Coyote Tales*, 20–24; James Teit, "Pend d'Oreille Tales," *Memoirs of the American Folk-Lore Society* 11 (1917): 114–18; James A. Teit et. al., *Folk-Tales of the Salishan and Sahaptin Tribes*, ed. by Franz Boas (Lancaster PA and New York: American Folk-Lore Society, 1917), 115; Louisa McDermott, "Folk-Lore of the Flathead Indians of Idaho: Adventures of Coyote," *Journal of American Folk-Lore* 14 (Oct.–Dec. 1901): 240–51 (hereafter cited as McDermott, "Folk-Lore"); McDermott (1904); Duncan McDonald, "Indian Legend: How Missoula Got Its Name," *Bitterroot Journal* (Victor MT) 4 (Jan. 1978): 25; Carling Malouf, "Flathead Places and Placenames" (unpub. MS, copy at Salish-Pend d'Oreille Culture Committee, n.d.). Hereafter cited as Malouf, "Flathead Places and Placenames." Archaeologists found evidence showing Snłpú to be an ancient camping area, and Malouf, among others, decried the development and home building in the area after World War II.

Sources on placename Člmé: SPCC wi: Steve Egesdal and Felicite McDonald, 6/26/1998 and Steve Egesdal with John Peter Paul, June 1998; elders meeting on this book, 09/09/2002. Other sources: Sam Resurrection, NA CCF-60917-23-Flat-052. John Ewers, *Gustavus Sohon's Portraits of Flathead and Pend d'Oreille Indians, 1854* (Washington DC: Smithsonian Miscellaneous Collections, vol. 110, 1948), reported that Salish elder Pete Pichette said that the Flathead name for this place meant "Where the Trees Have No Lower Limbs." In the 1930s anthropologist Claude Schaeffer recorded the name of this place as "chilme" (Glenbow, microfilm reel 5; also AMNH, 2-54). For references to site, see also Isaac Stevens papers relevant to treaty; some basic documents are gathered in Robert Bigart and Clarence Woodcock, *In the Name of the Salish and Kootenai Nation: The 1855 Hell Gate Treaty and the Origin of the Flathead Indian Reservation* (Pablo, MT: Salish Kootenai College Press, 1996).

For Ncx̣ʷoteẃs: SPCC OHA audio tapes: Pete Beaverhead, 18/1 (1975); Pete Beaverhead, 48/2 (1975). SPCC wi: Agnes Paul and John Peter Paul, August 29, 1995 and September 6, 1995; Chauncey Beaverhead, August 5, 1995; Steve Egesdal and Felicite McDonald, June 26, 1998; Steve Egesdal with John Peter Paul, June 1998; Louie Adams, 2003; Louie Adams and Felicite McDonald in elders meeting to review this book, 01-28-2004.

The larger area of Grass Valley, where Člme is located, is called Nmlsé (Place of Cottonwoods). SPCC wi: Louie Adams, September 23, 2003.

"Jocko or Flathead Indian Reservation": From the reservation's establishment in 1855 until sometime after 1900, the reservation was commonly referred to by non-Indians as either the Jocko Reservation or the Flathead Reservation. There was no particular pattern to this use and no term seems to have clearly predominated, although Flathead seems to have been used more in official government documents. The term *Jocko* Reservation was used because the southernmost valley of the reservation—the location of the Flathead Agency headquarters and the area closest to the city of Missoula—was called the Jocko Valley (after Jacques "Jocko" Finley (1768–1828), a fur trapper who had numerous descendants among the Salish and other tribes in the region). The term *Flathead* Reservation was used because the confederation of tribes that signed the Hellgate Treaty—the Flathead (Salish), Pend d'Oreille, and Kootenai—were collectively referred to by U.S. officials as the Flathead Nation. Also, the lake that dominates the northern section of the reservation is called Flathead Lake. There are numerous explanations, all with some evidentiary basis but none conclusively proven, for the origin of the term *Flathead* in the early nineteenth century. Gradually, during the early twentieth century, "Jocko" Reservation fell into disuse and "Flathead" Reservation became the more commonly used name.

Sources on placename Nⱡʔaycčstm: SPCC OHA video: Agnes Paul (with Josephine Quequesah) and Joe Cullooyah, field trip to Missoula area, May 2000 (TPO tape ET102/ET103). SPCC wi: John Peter Paul, June 19, 1997; Lucy Vanderburg, January 5, 1996; John Peter Paul and Agnes Paul, September 6, 1995; SPCC elders meeting February 20, 1997; Steve Egesdal, Felicite McDonald, and Chauncey Beaverhead June 26, 1998; Steve Egesdal work w/ John Peter Paul on placenames, June 1998; Louie Adams (w/ John Peter Paul) April 21, 1997. Other sources: AMNH, I-95 to I-97. Some elders say the photo of the woman peeling bitterroot does not appear to be Mary Kaltomee (Sackwoman), but her granddaughter, Harriet Whitworth, positively identified the woman in the photo as being her *yayaʔ (maternal grandmother)* (elders review of draft, 01-29-2004).

Sources on placename Sloʔté: SPCC OHA audio tapes: Eneas Pierre, 39/2 (1975); Pete Beaverhead, 48/2 (1975); Eneas Pierre, 58/1 (1975); Eneas Pierre, 65/1 (1975). SPCC wi: John Peter Paul, September 6, 1995; John Peter Paul and Felicite McDonald, Elders placename meeting, December 4, 1997; Steve Egesdal, Felicite McDonald, and Chauncey Beaverhead, June 26, 1998; Steve Egesdal with Felicite McDonald, December 4, 2000. Other sources: Malouf, field notes, interview of Eneas Granjo recorded with Bert Hansen, November 19, 1949; George Weisel, Missou-

la MT, personal interview notes; AMNH, notes on Paul Antoine, I-177 to I-235.

Sources on placename Nʔaycčstm: SPCC OHA audio tapes: Pete Beaverhead, 18/1 (1975). SPCC wi: Eneas Vanderburg and other elders, elders meeting, October 31, 1995; John Peter Paul and Agnes Paul, September 6, 1995; Steve Egesdal and Felicite McDonald, June 26, 1998; Steve Egesdal and John Peter Paul, June 1998. Other sources: Joseph Giorda, S.J. et al., *Dictionary of the Kalispel or Flathead Indian Language* (St. Ignatius: St. Ignatius Print, 1877-79), 18; Eneas Granjo (UM, Paul Phillips papers, Box 4, File 4-17 (Flathead Litigation, No. 61—Miscellaneous), 1951); Duncan McDonald, *Weekly Missoulian*, October 31, 1884; Malouf, "Flathead Places and Place Names."

Sources on placename Qaⱡsá, or Epⱡítxʷeʔ: SPCC OHA video: SPCC field trip, September 17, 1997. SPCC OHA audio tapes: Eneas Pierre, 39/2 (1975). SPCC wi: Agnes Paul, February 20, 1997; Agnes Paul and other Salish elders, March 20, 1997; Agnes Paul, February 1997; Joe Cullooyah, February 25, 1997; Felicite McDonald, January 6, 1997, February 12, 1997; Felicite McDonald and Shirley Trahan, November 20, 2003; Louie Adams, 2003; Steve Egesdal and Felicite McDonald, June 26, 1998; Chauncey Beaverhead, April 28, 1998. Other sources: Eneas Granjo (UM, Paul Phillips papers, Box 4, File 4-17 (Flathead Litigation, No. 61—Miscellaneous), 1951); James Teit, "The Salishan Tribes of the Western Plateaus," ed. by Franz Boas, *45th Annual Report of the Bureau of American Ethnology* 45 (1927–28): 311 (hereafter cited as Teit, "Salishan Tribes"); Glenbow, microfilm reel 5. The Smtiʔus, the Salishan people whom Teit says were based in this area, were later apparently wiped out by epidemics of smallpox or other introduced diseases.

Sources on placename Smʔtu Sx̣ʷcuʔsʔ: spcc wi: Elders field trip to Blackfoot Valley, May 2003. Other sources: Arthur L. Stone, *Following Old Trails* (1911; repr. Missoula MT: Pictorial Histories, 1996), 97 and 99; Malouf, "Flathead Places and Placenames."

Sources on placename Tmsmɫi: spcc wi: Felicite McDonald, elders placenames meeting, December 4, 1997; elders meeting on this book, September 11, 2002. Other sources: Salish elder Pete Pichette's telling of the Coyote story relating to Tmsmɫi was written up in three sources: "Indian Legend: Why There Are No Salmon in Lolo Creek," *Bitterroot Journal* (Ronan MT) 4 (Dec. 1978): 24–25 (hereafter cited as Pichette, *Indian Legend*); "Coyote Stocks the Streams with Salmon," in Pichette, *Coyote Tales*, 16–18; and "Why There Are No Salmon in Lolo Creek," in Clark, *Indian Legends*, 98–100. For another version of this story, as well as information on the Lolo Trail, origin of the name "Lolo," and details regarding the Lewis and Clark expedition, see also Wheeler, *Trail of Lewis and Clark*, 78–80.

Ellen Bigsam's short version of the story, as interpreted by her son, Joe Bigsam, was written up by George Weisel and published as "Why the Flathead Have No Salmon" in *Ten Animal Myths*, 10–11. Weisel also mentioned the story in "Animal Names, Anatomical Terms, and Some Ethnozoology of the Flathead Indians," *Journal of the Washington Academy of Sciences* 42 (Nov. 1952): 345–55. See also Malouf, "Flathead Places and Place Names"; Gregory Mengarini, *Recollections of the Flathead Mission, Containing Brief Observations both Ancient and Contemporary Concerning this Particular Nation*, translated, edited, and with a biographical introduction by Glori T. Lothrop (Glendale CA: Arthur H. Clark, 1977); and Roberta Carkeek Cheney, *Names on the Face of Montana* (Missoula MT: University of Montana Publications in History, 1971).

The English placename *Lolo* comes from the Salish pronunciation of the name *Lawrence*, apparently in reference to a mixed-heritage trapper and hunter who lived in the area and was buried near Grave Creek.

Sources on placename Naptnišá: spcc oha audio tapes: Louise Vanderburg, 8/1 (1975). spcc wi: Louie Adams and Felicite McDonald, March 6, 2002; Steve Egesdal fax February 3, 1999; Elders meeting on this book, September 11, 2002. Other sources: The Nez Perce term for the Lolo Trail can be found in Haruo Aoki and Nez Perce Elders, *Nez Perce Dictionary*, University of California Publications in Linguistics 122 (Berkeley: University of California Press, 1992), 292. Meriwether Lewis's reference to the Nez Perce word for the trail can be found, for example, in Moulton 8, 85. Clark also remarked that the Salish told of some of our people traveling all the way to the Pacific Coast the previous year, 1804. See Moulton 5, 197.

Sources on placename Sntʔm̌čqey: spcc oha audio tapes: Pete Pierre, 52/2b (1975). spcc wi: Felicite McDonald, language camp, July 15, 1999. Other sources: See Malouf, "Flathead Places and Placenames," and Cheney, *Names on the Face of Montana*, 142.

Sources on placename Ep Smɫi: spcc oha audio tapes: Little Mary Finley, 46/2 (1975). spcc wi: Mike Durglo Sr., language camp, July 15, 1999; elders meeting on this book, September 11, 2002. Other sources: Malouf, field notes recorded with Bert Hansen, at Arlee MT, Nov. 19, 1949; Pichette, *Indian Legend*.

Sources on placename Nstetčcxʷétkʷ: SPCC wi: Felicite "Jim" McDonald, March 8, 2002; John Peter Paul at SPCC elders meeting February 20, 1997; elders meeting on this book, September 11, 2002; elder language meeting, 03-01-2004. Other sources: Paul Antoine quoted in AMNH, Flathead Notes 1, 1-184, and Glenbow, microfilm reel 5. Also from Duncan McDonald, as relayed by Arthur L. Stone in *Following Old Trails*, 154. McDonald, in an article in *New North-West* that was reprinted in the *Weekly Missoulian*, October 31, 1884, said "the original or aboriginal name of Bitter Root is In-chi-tzog-tay-tque"—apparently an attempt by McDonald to render Nstetčcxʷétkʷ. Some elders today prefer the word Nstetčcxʷkʷ.

Variants of this placename have been mentioned in a number of non-Indian sources. Stone said the word meant "Willow river," and wrote it out as "In-tschu-tet-tschu;" he said his spelling of the suffix "tschu" was rendered as "etiku" by the Jesuit priest and historian Lawrence Palladino, who said it meant "water." See Palladino, *Indian and White in the Northwest; or, A History of Catholicity in Montana* (Baltimore: John Murphy, 1894), 313–14. Pallidino's suffix is clearly, in IPA, the suffix -etkʷ, which does indeed connote water. Stone's word, "In-tschu-tet-tschu," would probably be rendered, in IPA, as something like Ntcčxʷtetcčxʷ, and is probably just a garbling of the actual Salish placename Nstetčcxʷetkʷ.

Given the tendency in Salish-Pend d'Oreille ethnogeography to identify small streams, but not entire large rivers, by a single name, it is possible that non-Indian researchers like Stone or Schaeffer may have insistently asked for a name for the Bitterroot River, and may have finally been given one—more to satisfy their apparent need for a word than because it was a genuine Salish placename. This pos-

sibility may also apply to another supposed name for the Bitterroot River mentioned in Wheeler, *Trail of Lewis and Clark*, 76. Wheeler claimed that "The Salish Indian name for the Bitterroot River is *Spitlem sulkn*, the water of the Bitter Root, and the valley is called *Spitlemen*, the place of the Bitter Root." Wheeler was trying to represent *Speȼm Sewɬkʷ*, which would literally mean Bitterroot waters—in all likelihood a back-translation into Salish of the English placename Bitterroot River, rather than a genuine Salish placename.

Sources on placename Łq̇éɬml̓š: SPCC OHA audio tapes: Eneas Pierre, 13/2 and 58/1 (1975). SPCC wi: Felicite McDonald, July 25, 1995, and September 19, 2001; Chauncey Beaverhead, January 14, 2000; elders meeting on this book, September 11, 2002; Joe Vanderburg, July 25, 2003. Other sources: AMNH, 1-95 to 1-97; Glenbow, microfilm reel 5; Teit, "Salishan Tribes," 310; William L. Davis, S.J., *A History of St. Ignatius Mission* (Spokane WA: C. W. Hill, 1954), 5; Mengarini, *Recollections of the Flathead Mission*, 191; Cheney, *Names on the Face of Montana*, 210–11.

Sources on placename Čkʷlkʷlqéyn: SPCC OHA audio tapes: Eneas Pierre, 13/2 (1975). SPCC wi: Felicite McDonald and Steve Egesdal, placenames review June 26, 1998; Felicite McDonald, December 12, 1996; Louie Adams and Eneas Vanderburg, elders meeting on this book, September 11, 2002 and 01-29-2004; see also Felicite McDonald's notes on Bitterroot Placenames handwritten in her copy of SPCC *Common Names*.

Sources on placename Čɬčlčlé: SPCC wi: Agnes Paul, Mike Durglo Sr., Eneas Vanderburg, and Felicite McDonald (language camp), July 15, 1999; Felicite McDonald, October 15, 2003; Joe Vanderburg, July 25, 2003 and October

15, 2003; elders meeting on this book, September 11, 2002 and 01-29-2004; see also Myrna Adams's map in SPCC archives; see also Felicite McDonald's notes on Bitterroot Placenames handwritten in her copy of SPCC *Common Names*: "sʔatqʷɬp corral for elk."

Sources on placename Sq̓x̣q̓x̣ó: SPCC OHA audio tapes: Eneas Pierre, 65/1 (1975). SPCC wi: Felicite McDonald, September 5, 1997 and March 4, 2002; elders meeting on this book, September 11, 2002 and 1-29-2004. Some elders pronounce this placename without the s, as Q̓x̣q̓x̣ó. Other sources: For a discussion of the "beaver" theory of the word's etymology, see undated newspaper clipping in SPCC file on Bitterroot placenames, which draws from Father Grassi's dictionary of the Salish language.

Isaac Stevens stated in October 1855, in the Judith River treaty negotiations, that the "Western Indians go to Buffalo on the other side of the Missouri. They use certain passes. The Medicine Rock, the Big Hole, and others further south." In Albert J. Partoll, ed., "The Blackfoot Indian Peace Council: A Document of the Official Proceedings of a treaty Between the Blackfoot Nation and Other Indians and the United States, in October, 1855," *Frontier and Midland* 17 (Spring 1937): 201. For references to buffalo in the Drummond/Flint Creek area west of the mountains in 1840s, see Warren E. Ferris, *Life in the Rocky Mountains* (Denver: The Old West, 1940).

Sources on placename Snetetšé: SPCC OHA audio tapes: Agnes Vanderburg, 1/2 (1975); Charlie McDonald, 167/2 (1978); Louise Vanderburg, Agnes Vanderburg, Joe Eneas, and Eneas Pierre, 189/2 (1979); Pete Pierre, 260/2 (1981). SPCC wi: see Felicite McDonald's notes on Bitterroot Placenames handwritten in her copy of SPCC *Common*

Names. Other sources: Pichette, *Coyote Tales*, 34–38; McDermott, "Folk-Lore"; McDermott (1904).

Sources on placename Snk̓ʷɬxʷexʷemí: SPCC OHA audio tapes: Eneas Pierre, 1/2, 13/2, 52/2 A (all 1975). SPCC wi: from field trip to Bitterroot, June 1996; Louie Adams, elders meeting on this book, September 11, 2002.

Sources on placename Snam̓šá: SPCC OHA audio tapes: Pete Pierre, 52/2 (1975). SPCC wi: Louie Adams and Felicite McDonald, March 6, 2002; elders meeting on this book, September 11, 2002 and 1-29-2004 (note that some elders pronounce this placename without the "s," as Nam̓šá); see also Myrna Adams's map in SPCC archives.

Sources on placename Čq̓ʔé: SPCC OHA audio tapes: Eneas Pierre and Pete Woodcock, 1/2 (1975). SPCC wi: Felicite McDonald, March 8, 2002. Other sources: Pichette, *Coyote Tales*, 64–66.

Sources on placename K̓ʷtiɬ P̓upm̓: SPCC wi: Louie Adams, January 28, 2001 and October 3, 2000; elders meeting to review this book, 1-29-2004. Other sources: In Clark, *Indian Legends*, 143, elder Pete Pichette is quoted as calling this place Cutl-kkh-pooh. As we note in the text, linguistic and ethnogeographic work with tribal elders and linguists suggests Clark was probably trying to write a Salish placename that would be rendered as K̓ʷtiɬ P̓u (short form), or K̓ʷtiɬ P̓upm̓ (long form), in the International Phonetic Alphabet. This placename means coming out into a big open place. Other elders have also suggested that when the white writer transcribed Pichette as saying "Cutl-kkh-pooh," the actual Salish word was not K̓ʷtiɬ P̓u, but Suɬkʷpú—meaning downhill. This was because from Ross's Hole, you would travel downhill, downstream to the Bitterroot Valley, to get to the main encampments of the Salish. Some families may have used this word to refer to the area. Different families had different names for many of the traditional places.

Wheeler, *Trail of Lewis and Clark*, 61–63, said that the trails linking the area to the Bitterroot Valley, according to Wheeler, ran just west of Cameron Creek, the northwest trail splitting and leading into the Bitterroot in two places—the "wagon bridge near Wilde's Spring" and *via* the Rye Creek drainage. By taking these routes, travelers could avoid the narrow canyon of the East Fork of the Bitterroot. Wheeler also mentioned "the old Indian trail" that passed from the Camp Creek area across "the mountain to Wisdom River." Wheeler said this was a "characteristic one, broad and winding. At the summit, as is usual, it scattered into many parallel trails. At places it now forms a part of the wagon road. . . . The girdled and bark-stripped pine trees are a mute testimony to the former presence of the Indians, who habitually ate the delicate inner lining of the tree" (pp. 318–19).

Sources on placename Skʷumcné Sewłkʷs: SPCC OHA audio tapes: Pete Beaverhead, 44/1 (1975). SPCC WI: Louie Adams, January 28, 2001 and October 3, 2000. Other sources: Victor Vanderburg and Paul Antoine, Glenbow, microfilm reel 5. SPCC telephone communication with USFS biologist, Wisdom Ranger district, September 2002.

The Beginning of the Great Changes

1. There is an enormous literature on the demographic impact of early epidemics of European diseases on Native American peoples, and a wide-ranging debate over precontact population levels. Virtually all contemporary scholars have revised upward, in dramatic terms, the first estimates of pre-Columbian populations developed by anthropologists such as John Moody (*The Aboriginal Population of America North of Mexico*, ed. by J. S. Swanton (Smithsonian Miscellaneous Collections 80(7), Washington DC, 1928), but there remain wide disparities in the scholarship. Some of the highest population estimates came from *Their Numbers Become Thinned: Native American Population Dynamics in Eastern North America* (Knoxville: University of Tennessee Press, 1983), Henry Dobyns's seminal work in the field. Dobyns wrote that native populations throughout the Americas were radically reduced by the spread of smallpox in the sixteenth century after its introduction into Mexico by the Spanish conquistadors. Since Dobyns, most historians and anthropologists have arrived at lower figures, but still much higher than the first estimates. Some researchers have been less committal in estimating population numbers but have, at the same time, argued for far-reaching impacts from these epidemics and for an extensive reevaluation of early Native American history (e.g., Daniel T. Reff, *Disease, Depopulation, and Culture Change in Northwestern New Spain, 1518–1764*. Salt Lake City: University of Utah Press, 1991). For a popular overview of the scholarly research and disagreements over this issue, see Charles C. Mann, "1491," *The Atlantic Monthly*, March 2002: 41–53.

For the Salish in particular, the low figures of Moody and other early anthropological demographers were challenged by some ethnographers, particularly Teit, "Salishan Tribes." Teit estimated the pre-white population of the Salish and Pend d'Oreille at fifteen-thousand. He based his figure on rudimentary knowledge of the extent and impact of smallpox and other diseases before the arrival of Lewis and Clark. One of the earliest works to focus on this issue in this region was Leslie M. Scott, "Indian Diseases as Aids to Pacific Northwest Settlement," *Oregon Historical Quarterly* 29 (2) (1928): 144–61.

A number of researchers have in recent years combined more advanced methods of population and disease analysis with a rigorous reexamination of archival sources to develop revised population estimates. See, for example, R. T. Boyd, *The Introduction of Infectious Diseases among the Indians of the Pacific Northwest, 1774–1874* (PhD diss., University of Washington, Seattle, 1985). Boyd also wrote the chapter on "Demographic History until 1990" in *Handbook of North American Indians*, vol. 12: Plateau (Washington DC: Smithsonian Institution, 1998), 467–83. Where earlier scholars tended to rely almost solely on the shaky head counts of early white visitors to tribal territories, historical demographers like Boyd have employed a far wider range of evidence, including analysis of shifting land use patterns as reflected in fire histories, records relating to the spread of horses and intertribal territories, and perhaps most importantly, tribal oral histories. Sarah K. Campbell's archaeological work has uncovered evidence of sudden disruptions in life in the Middle Columbia Plateau in the mid-1500s, which she suggests may be the result of massive mortality from epidemics in the region at that early date. See Campbell, "Post-Columbian Culture History in the Northern Columbia Plateau: A.D. 1500–1900" (PhD diss., University of Washington, Seattle, 1989). Cole Harris, "Voices of Disaster: Smallpox around the Strait of Georgia in 1782," *Ethnohistory* 41 (4) (Fall 1994): 591–627, is also an important study of the impact of smallpox epidemics in the region prior to 1800.

This mounting body of scholarship has made clear that by the early nineteenth century, epidemics had already been wreaking havoc among tribal populations for at least decades and perhaps even for centuries. Yet, until the late nineteenth century, actual population counts and figures were scattered and largely anecdotal, issuing from informal observations made by non-Indian explorers, fur trappers, traders, and missionaries, including Lewis and Clark, LeBlanc and LeGasse, and others. As such, they provide a sketchy basis for estimating pre-disease populations. See Claude E. Schaeffer, "LeBlanc and LeGasse: Predecessors of David Thompson in the Columbia Plateau," in *Studies in Plains Anthropology* 3 (Browning MT: Museum of the Plains Indian, Indian Arts and Crafts Board, U.S. Department of the Interior, 1966). Other sources include David Thompson, *David Thompson's Journals Relating to Montana and Adjacent Regions, 1808–1812*, ed. and with an introduction by M. Catherine White (Missoula MT: Montana State University Press, 1950) (hereafter *David Thompson's Journals Relating to Montana*); Alexander Ross, *Adventures of the First Settlers on the Oregon or Columbia River*, edited by Milo Milton Quaife (Chicago: Lakeside Press, R. R. Donnelly and Sons, 1923); George Simpson, *Fur Trade and Empire: George Simpson's Journal*, ed. by Frederick Merk (Cambridge MA: The Belknap Press of Harvard University, 1968); Warren Ferris, *Life in the Rocky Mountains*, ed. by Paul C. Phillips (Denver CO: The Old West, 1940); John McClellan, as described in Harry M. Majors, "John McClellan in the Montana Rockies 1807: The First Americans after Lewis and Clark," *Northwest Discovery* 2 (19): 554–630; Mengarini, *Recollections of the Flathead Mission*; and Isaac Stevens, *Reports of explorations and surveys to ascertain the most practicable and economical route for a railroad from the Mississippi river to the Pacific Ocean* (Washington DC: Thomas H. Ford, for the House of Representatives, 33rd Congress, 2nd Session, Ex. Doc. no. 91, vol. 1., 1855).

Our own estimates of the combined Salish-Pend d'Oreille population—a range of between twenty-thousand and sixty-thousand before the diseases struck, and between two-thousand and eight-thousand by about 1800—are developed from a review of all these materials and surveys of the resource base that sustained the tribes. These population estimates encompass bands and groups throughout the vast pre-1700 original aboriginal territories of both tribes, ranging from the Musselshell country in the east to the Pend d'Oreille River in the west. We emphasize that these are only informed estimates, and that more work needs to be done in this important area of research.

2. Louie Adams, SPCC WI, October 3, 2000.

The Question of Intent

1. For Jefferson's instructions to Lewis, see Donald Jackson, ed., *Letters of the Lewis and Clark Expedition with Related Documents, 1783–1854*, 2nd ed., vol. 1 (Urbana, Chicago, and London: University of Illinois Press, 1978), 61 (hereafter cited as Jackson vol. 1). See also Lewis to Clark, June 19, 1803, Jackson vol. 1, 57. For Jefferson's confidential letter to Congress of January 18, 1803, see Jackson, vol. 1, 10–13.

2. Jackson vol. 1, 10–13.

3. Clark, see Moulton 5: 188; Ordway, see Moulton 9, 219; Whitehouse, see Moulton, 11, 301.

James Ronda has noted that Lewis and Clark's speeches to tribes followed a general pattern: they "began with a grand announcement of American sovereignty over the newly purchased lands" of Louisiana territory. In other words, they began their communications with statements based on western notions of nation-states and land ownership that would have been difficult if not impossible for many tribal people to understand. Lewis or Clark would then explain their intention of establishing peace in order to allow commerce to grow. They would explain where they were going and then engage in trading and discussion of matters of particular interest to each specific tribe. As Ronda's scholarship has made clear, the main message taken by many Missouri River tribes was that the United States would now replace Spain or France as their primary non-Indian trading partner. James P. Ronda, *Lewis and Clark among the Indians* (Lincoln: University of Nebraska Press, 1984): 18–19. See also *Voyages of Discovery: Essays on the Lewis and Clark Expedition*, ed. and with an introduction and afterword by James P. Ronda (Helena: Montana Historical Society), 1998.

4. Clark, apparently to George Rogers Clark, September 23, 1806, in Jackson vol. 1, 326.

5. Jackson vol. 1, 327.

6. Lewis, September 29, 1806, in Jackson vol. 1, 339.

7. *Weekly Missoulian*, April 26, 1876.

8. Bud Barnaby on Tony Charlo's story of Sacajawea's grave: SPCC WI, September 16, 1998.

To Help Them or to Wipe Them Out

1. Nez Perce elders recall that among their people, leaders also debated whether or not to wipe out the strangers and only narrowly decided to spare them. See Clark, *Indian Legends*, 69–72.

"The chief immediately sent his warriors to meet the strange men and bring them to camp safely": Pete Pichette, in Clark, *Indian Legends*, 143–45. Used with permission of the University of Oklahoma Press. The Salish placename that Clark records as "Cutl-kkh-pooh" is $K^{w}tít$ Pu, a shortened form of $K^{w}tít$ $Pupím$. See also placename $K^{w}tít$ $Pupím$, p. 76 of this volume. To some extent, Clark's accuracy in transcribing Salish words can be assessed by comparing her rendering of this placename with her rendering of the Salish name of the chief at the time of the encounter with the expedition, which she writes as *Tchlis-ka-e-mee*. This is recognizably close to the correct name, *Čełl Sq̇ey̓mí*, meaning Three Eagles.

"She said they were concerned when they saw them, because they had a $q^{w}ásq^{w}i?$ with them": Louie Adams, SPCC OHA video, August 2001.

"Sophie Moiese said if it wasn't for York, they would have wiped out that party": Joe Vanderburg, SPCC OHA, mini-disc, August 2003.

Gift-giving and Confusion

1. Moulton 11, 344.

"They didn't know that camas roots are good to eat": Sophie Moiese, in Clark, *Indian Legends,* 145n.

"At a distance he saw a party of about twenty men traveling toward his camp": Francois Saxa, retelling a story told him by Agnes, the widow of Chief Victor; Saxa told his story in 1899 to Fr. Jerome D'Aste, who waited three days, and then sent it to O. D. Wheeler, who printed it in *Trail of Lewis and Clark*, vol. 2, 65–68. Wheeler said he himself made "a change here and there" (see comments on pp. 136–37). A version of D'Aste's letter also appears in Clark, *Indian Legends,* 145–47.

Lewis and Clark in the Fold of Tribal History

1. NA 75, BIA LR 1893–1837.

2. Lewis to Jefferson, September 23, 1806, in Jackson vol. 1, 321–22.

3. Perhaps a stronger argument can be made for the expedition's direct impact on the southwestward expansion of the British-Canadian fur trade. Lewis, for example, did write a letter in 1806 to the Canadian trader and explorer David Thompson summarizing the expedition, and Thompson referred repeatedly to the expedition in his journals. See, for example, *David Thompson's Journals Relating to Montana*, vii and 203–204.

4. Hoecken, in Bigart and Woodcock, "In the Name of the Salish & Kootenai Nation," 141–48. Throughout the nineteenth century, tribal leaders repeatedly asserted that the Flathead Reservation, as it was explained and "pointed out" to them in 1855, was supposed to encompass far more land than is embraced within the modern-day reservation boundaries. The northern and western boundaries, especially, were contested by tribal members. In the Northern Pacific Railroad right-of-way negotiations of 1882 and in numerous letters of protest over the planned opening of the reservation to white settlement after passage of the Flathead Allotment Act in 1904, tribal leaders asserted that the northern boundary of the reservation, as it had been interpreted to them in 1855, was supposed to be the Canadian line.

5. In the years after the war, a number of Nez Perce from Chief Joseph's band, who had escaped into Canada under the leadership of White Bird, did accept the Salish offer and moved to the Flathead Reservation.

6. According to information printed on the back of this photograph in the MHS collection (photo no. 941-737), this is an image of Tzi-kal-tza, the [Nez Perce or Salish] son of William Clark. It was donated to the Montana Historical Society by a prominent early Montanan, Nathaniel Pitt Langford, who said he arranged to have the picture taken in 1866 or 1867 "in Montana." Langford said the identification of the image was confirmed by Granville Stuart, who claimed that he "knew the old man well." Tzi-kal-tza would have been about sixty years old at the time the photograph was taken. The name Tzi-kal-tza was provided by Duncan McDonald. McDonald was a member of the Confederated Salish and Kootenai Tribes, but he was partly Nez Perce and married to a Nez Perce woman, so it is unclear whether Tzi-kal-tza is a name in the Salish or Nez Perce language.

7. Pete Beaverhead, SPCC OHA 68/2 (1975).

Selected Bibliography

Oral History Collections (*not open to the general public*)

Salish-Pend d'Oreille Culture Committee, Confederated Salish and Kootenai Tribes. St. Ignatius MT.

Manuscript and Photographic Collections

American Museum of Natural History, New York NY. Claude Schaeffer papers.

Coe Collection of Western Americana, Beinecke Rare Book Library, Yale University, New Haven CT. Photographic records and various records relating to the Flathead Reservation.

D'Arcy McNickle Library, Salish Kootenai College, Pablo MT. Photographic collections and various records relating to the Flathead Reservation.

Glenbow Institute, Calgary, Alberta. Claude Schaeffer collection, microfilm reels.

Jesuit Oregon Province Archives, Gonzaga University, Spokane WA.

Milwaukee Public Museum, Milwaukee WI. Photographic collections.

Montana Historical Society Archives, Helena MT. Photographic collections and various records relating to the Flathead Reservation.

National Archives, Washington DC, documents from Record Group 75 (Bureau of Indian Affairs), letters received by the BIA (1881–1907) and Central Classified Files (after 1907).

National Archives, Rocky Mountain Regional Federal Record Center, Denver CO. Flathead Agency records.

Ravalli County Museum/Bitter Root Valley Historical Society, Hamilton MT. Photographic collections and various records relating to the Salish people.

Swan Valley Ecosystem Center, Condon MT. Photographic collections and various records relating to Salish and Pend d'Oreille tribal members.

University of Montana Archives and Special Collections, Missoula MT. Photographic collections and various records relating to the Flathead Reservation.

University of Pennsylvania, Philadelphia PA. Photographic collections.

Secondary Sources

Alt, David. *Glacial Lake Missoula and Its Humongous Floods*. Missoula: Mountain Press, 2001.

Aoki, Haruo, and Nez Perce Elders. *Nez Perce Dictionary*. University of California Publication in Linguistics, 122. Berkeley: University of California Press, 1992.

Bigart, Robert, and Clarence Woodcock. *In the Name of the Salish and Kootenai Nation: The 1855 Hell Gate Treaty and the Origin of the Flathead Indian Reservation*. Pablo MT: Salish Kootenai College Press, 1996.

Boyd, R. T. "Demographic History until 1990." In *Handbook of North American Indians*. Vol. 12, *Plateau*, ed. Deward E. Walker, Jr., 467–83. Washington DC: Smithsonian Institution, 1998.

———. "The Introduction of Infectious Diseases among the Indians of the Pacific Northwest, 1774–1874." PhD dissertation, Dept. of Anthropology, University of Washington, Seattle, 1985.

Campbell, Sarah K. "Post-Columbian Culture History in the Northern Columbia Plateau: A.D. 1500–1900." PhD dissertation, Dept. of Anthropology, University of Washington, Seattle, 1989.

Cheney, Roberta Carkeek. *Names on the Face of Montana*. Missoula MT: University of Montana Publications in History, 1971.

Clark, Ella E. "George Gibbs' Account of the Indian Mythology of Oregon and Washington Territories." *Oregon Historical Quarterly* 56, no. 4 (Dec. 1955): 293–325.

———. *Indian Legends from the Northern Rockies*. 4th ed. Norman: Oklahoma University Press, 1977.

———. "Sesquicentennial Remembrances: The Lewis and Clark Expedition as Seen through the Eyes of the Indians in the Northern Rocky Mountains." *Montana: the Magazine of Western History* 5, no. 2 (1955): 31–39.

Curtis, Edward S. *The North American Indian*. Vol. 7. 1911. Reprint New York: Johnson Reprint Corporation, 1976.

Davis, William L., S.J. *History of St. Ignatius Mission*. Spokane WA: C. W. Hill Printing Company, 1954.

Dobyns, Henry. *Their Numbers Become Thinned: Native American Population Dynamics in Eastern North America*. Knoxville: University of Tennessee Press, 1983.

Ewers, John. *Gustavus Sohon's Portraits of Flathead and Pend d'Oreille Indians, 1854*. Smithsonian Miscellaneous Collections. Vol. 110, No. 7. Washington DC: Smithsonian Institution, 1948.

Ferris, Warren E. *Life in the Rocky Mountains*. Denver CO: The Old West Publishing Company, 1940.

Giorda, Joseph, S.J., et al. *A Dictionary of the Kalispel or Flathead Indian Language*. Compiled by the Missionaries of the Society of Jesus. 2 vols. St. Ignatius MT: St. Ignatius Print, 1877–79.

Hansen, Bert. " 'Your Land Forever': Lewis and Clark Sesquicentennial, Council Grove Treaty Centennial, U.S. Forest Service 50th Birthday. August 12–13–14, 1955." Mimeo, n.p. Missoula MT, 1955.

Harris, Cole. "Voices of Disaster: Smallpox around the Strait of Georgia in 1782." *Ethnohistory* 41, no. 4 (Fall 1994): 591–627.

Hoffman, W. J. "Selish Myths." *Bulletin of the Essex Institute* 15 (1883): 23–40.

Jackson, Donald, ed. *Letters of the Lewis and Clark Expedition with Related Documents, 1783–1854*, 2nd edition. 2 vols. Urbana: University of Illinois Press, 1978.

Lincoln, Mother Angela. *Life of the Rev. Mother Amadeus of the Heart of Jesus: Foundress of the Ursuline Missions of Montana and Alaska*. New York: The Paulist Press, 1923.

Malouf, Carling. "The Coniferous Forests and Their Uses in the Northern Rocky Mountains through 9,000 Years of Prehistory." In *Forests of the Northern Rocky*

Mountains: Proceedings of the 1968 University of Montana Foundation, ed. Richard D. Taber, 271–90. Missoula: University of Montana Foundation, 1969.

———. "Flathead Places and Placenames." Unpublished MS, n.d. Copy at Salish-Pend d'Oreille Culture Committee, St. Ignatius MT.

McDermott, Louisa. "Ethnology and Folklore, Selish Proper." Master's Thesis, University of California–Berkeley, 1904.

———. "Folk-Lore of the Flathead Indians of Idaho: Adventures of Coyote." *Journal of American Folk-Lore* 14, no. 55 (October–December 1901): 240–51.

McDonald, Duncan. "Indian Legend: How Missoual Got Its Name." *Bitterroot Journal* (Victor MT) 4, no. 1 January 1978): 25.

McDonald, W. H. *Creation Tales from the Salish*. Billings MT: Montana Indian Publication Fund, 1973.

Mengarini, Gregory. *Recollections of the Flathead Mission, Containing Brief Observations both Ancient and Contemporary Concerning this Particular Nation*. Translated, edited, and with a biographical introduction by Gloria T. Lothrop. Glendale CA: Arthur H. Clark, 1977.

Miller, Harriet, and Elizabeth Harrison. *Coyote Tales of the Montana Salish*. From tales narrated by Pierre Pichette. Exhibition of Indian Arts and Crafts Board, U.S. Department of the Interior. Rapid City SD: The Tipi Shop, 1974.

Moulton, Gary, ed. *The Journals of the Lewis and Clark Expedition, Volume 1: Atlas of the Lewis and Clark Expedition*. Lincoln: University of Nebraska Press, 1983.

———, ed. *The Journals of the Lewis and Clark Expedition, Volume 5: July 28–November 1, 1805*. Lincoln: University of Nebraska Press, 1988.

———, ed. *The Journals of the Lewis and Clark Expedition, Volume 8: June 10–September 26, 1806*. Lincoln: University of Nebraska Press, 1993.

———, ed. *The Journals of the Lewis and Clark Expedition, Volume 9: The Journals of John Ordway, May 14, 1804–September 23, 1806, and Charles Floyd, May 14–August 18, 1804*. Lincoln: University of Nebraska Press, 1996.

———, ed. *The Journals of the Lewis and Clark Expedition, Volume 10: The Journal of Patrick Gass, May 14, 1804–September 23, 1806*. Lincoln: University of Nebraska Press, 1996.

———, ed. *The Journals of the Lewis and Clark Expedition, Volume 11: The Journals of Joseph Whitehouse, May 14, 1804–April 2, 1806*. Lincoln: University of Nebraska Press, 1997.

Owen, John. *The Journals and Letters of Major John Owen, 1850–1871*. Edited by Seymour Dunbar, and with notes to Owen's texts by Paul C. Phillips. 2 vols. New York: Eberstadt, 1927.

Palladino, Lawrence. *Indian and White in the Northwest; or, A History of Catholicity in Montana*. Baltimore: John Murphy and Company, 1894.

Patroll, Albert J., ed. "The Blackfoot Indian Peace Council: A Document of the Official Proceedings of a Treaty between the Blackfoot Nation and Other Indians and the United States, in October, 1855." *Frontier and Midland* 17 (Spring 1937): 199–207.

Peterson, Jacqueline, with Laura Peers. *Sacred Encounters: Father De Smet and the Indians of the Rocky Mountain West*. Norman and London: The De Smet Project, Washington State University, in association with University of Oklahoma Press, 1993.

Pichette, Pierre (Pete). "Indian Legend: Why There Are No Salmon in Lolo Creek." *Bitterroot Journal* (Victor MT) 4, no. 12 (December 1978): 24–25.

Reff, Daniel T. *Disease, Depopulation, and Culture Change in Northwestern New Spain, 1518–1764.* Salt Lake City: University of Utah Press, 1991.

Revais, Michel. "Pend d'Oreille Tales." As told to James A. Teit. *Memoirs of the American Folk-Lore Society* 11 (1917): 114–18.

Ronan, Peter. *History of the Flathead Indians.* Minneapolis: Ross & Haines, 1890.

Ronda, James P. *Lewis and Clark among the Indians.* Lincoln: University of Nebraska Press, 1984.

———, ed., introduction, and afterword. *Voyages of Discovery: Essays on the Lewis and Clark Expedition.* Helena: Montana Historical Society Press, 1998.

Schaeffer, Claude E. "LeBlanc and LeGasse: Predecessors of David Thompson in the Columbia Plateau." *Studies in Plains Anthropology* 3. Browning MT: Museum of the Plains Indian, Indian Arts and Crafts Board, U.S. Department of the Interior, 1966.

Scott, Leslie M. "Indian Diseases as Aids to Pacific Northwest Settlement." *Oregon Historical Quarterly* 29, no. 2 (1928): 144–61.

Smith, Thompson R. "History [of Flathead and Pend d'Oreille]." In *Handbook of North American Indians.* Vol. 12, *Plateau*, ed. Deward E. Walker Jr., 305–12. Washington DC: Smithsonian Institution, 1998.

———. "The Salish (*Séliš* or "Flathead") and Pend d'Oreille (*Qlispé*): History of Relations with Non-Indians." Author's final submission (pre-edited), 1997, for *Handbook of North American Indians*, Vol. 12, *Plateau*, ed. Deward E. Walker Jr. Washington DC: Smithsonian Institution, 1998.

Stone, Arthur. *Following Old Trails.* 1913. Reprint, Missoula MT: Pictorial Histories, 1996.

Swanton, J. S., ed. *The Aboriginal Population of America North of Mexico.* Smithsonian Miscellaneous Collections 80(7). Washington DC: Smithsonian Institution, 1928.

Teit, James. "Pend d'Oreille Tales." As told by Michel Revais. *Memoirs of the American Folk-Lore Society* 11 (1917): 114–18.

———. "The Salishan Tribes of the Western Plateaus." Ed. Franz Boas. *Forty-fifth Annual Report of the Bureau of American Ethnology for 1927–1928*: 295–396.

Teit, James A., et. al. *Folk-Tales of the Salishan and Sahaptin Tribes.* Ed. Franz Boas. Lancaster PA and New York: American Folk-Lore Society, 1917.

Thompson, David. *David Thompson's Journals Relating to Montana and Adjacent Regions, 1808–1812.* Ed. and with an introduction by M. Catherine White. Missoula: Montana State University Press, 1950.

Thwaites, Reuben G., ed. *Original Journals of the Lewis and Clark Expedition, 1804–1806.* 8 vols. New York: Dodd, Mead, and Company, 1904–1905.

Vanderburg, Agnes, Ignace Pierre, Jerome Lumpry, and Adele Adams. *Tales from the Bitterroot Valley, and Other Salish Folk Stories.* As told to Kathryn Law, interpreted by Agnes Vanderburg. Billings MT: Montana Indian Publications, 1971.

Weisel, George. *Ten Animal Myths of the Flathead Indians.* As told by Ellen Bigsam, interpreted by Joe Bigsam. *Anthropology and Sociology Papers* 18. Missoula: Montana State University (now University of Montana), 1959.

Wheeler, Olin D. *The Trail of Lewis and Clark, 1804–1904.* 2 vols. New York and London: G. P. Putnam's Sons, the Knickerbocker Press, 1904. Reprint AMS Press, New York, 1976.

Woody, Judge F. H. "A Sketch of the Early History of Western Montana." In *Contributions to the Historical Society of Montana.* Vol. 2: 1896. Reprint Boston: J. S. Canner and Company 1966, 88–106.

Index

Source Acknowledgments

Text Credits

Stories told by Pete Pichette on pages 93–94 and Sophie Moiese on page 102 appeared in Ella Clark, *Indian Legends from the Northern Rockies*, published by the University of Oklahoma Press. Copyright 1966 by the University of Oklahoma Press. Reprinted with permission.

Photo and Illustration Credits

Copyrights on images from the Salish-Pend d'Oreille Photographic Archives, Salish-Pend d'Oreille Culture Committee (SPCC and CSKT) are held by the Confederated Salish and Kootenai Tribes. Images from other sources are used with permission.

ix *10,000 Years Indigenous People—200 Years Lewis and Clark*, no. 6. Monoprint series—multimedia, 2001. By Corwin Clairmont. Courtesy of the artist. Photograph by Dirk Bakker, courtesy Eiteljorg Museum.

xi John Peter Paul. Photograph by Thompson Smith. SPCC.

xiii Julie Cahune, Tony Incashola, and Germaine White. Photograph by Thompson Smith. SPCC.

xvi Salish-Pend d'Oreille Elders Cultural Advisory Council. Photograph by Tony Incashola. SPCC.

1 *The Day Lewis and Clark Came.* Oil painting by Tony Sandoval. SPCC.

2 Mission Valley and Mission Mountains, 1884. "Flathead Valley, Montana." 1894. Photograph by F. Jay Haynes. Haynes Collection, H-4132. Courtesy Montana Historical Society.

3 Bitterroot River. Photograph by Thompson Smith. SPCC.

4 Josephine Camille and her daughter Lucy, Flathead Reservation, July 1906. 954-554. Courtesy Montana Historical Society.

5 Ceremonial Rings, located in Gallatin County on a plateau above the junction of the south fork and the north fork of Sixteen [Mile Creek] near Francis, June 1940. Photograph by John L. Maloney. 954-921. Courtesy Montana Historical Society.

6 Bitterroot River. Photograph by Todd Kaplan. Courtesy Todd Kaplan and the American Public Land Exchange Company, Missoula MT.

18 Salish encampment. Photograph by R. H. McKay. McKay Photograph Collection, 94-8. K. Ross Toole Archives. Courtesy University of Montana.

20 Unidentified Salish man. SPCC.

24 Elisepe and boy. Record group 75 (Bureau of Indian Affairs), Flathead Agency Records, C. C. Wright Desk Files, Box 63. Rocky Mountain Region Federal Records Center, Denver. Courtesy National Archives.

27 Cecille Kaiser and Anye Antoine. Photograph by Claude Schaeffer. Glenbow Archives, NA 5213-27. Courtesy Glenbow Museum, Calgary, Alberta, Canada.

27 Agnes Vanderburg. Photograph by Mildred Chaffin. M. Chaffin collection, Number 6. Courtesy Swan Ecosystem Center/Upper Swan Valley Historical Society, Condon MT.

28 Paul Antoine. Claude Schaeffer collection. Courtesy Division of Anthropology, American Museum of Natural History, New York.

Charlie Russell's *Lewis and Clark Meeting the Indians at Ross' Hole*

Charlie Russell's *Lewis and Clark Meeting the Indians at Ross' Hole*

An Appreciation

In 1912 the Montana legislature commissioned Charlie Russell to paint a massive mural to hang above the house chambers in the state capitol. The renowned cowboy artist surprised his patrons with a work that subverts the usual glorified view of the Lewis and Clark expedition. Rather than depicting the explorers in the conventional terms of heroic iconography, Russell has Lewis and Clark fading into the background, barely visible at the right edge of the painting. They seem to be negotiating a deal, perhaps haggling over the price of the horses they desperately needed. It is the Salish warriors, not the white explorers, whom Russell places front and center, in a classic equestrian pose—a dashing, dramatic charge, towering over the white interlop-

ers. The sweep and force of the warriors' movement across the enormous canvas suggests that history itself could have moved in an entirely different direction. And indeed, in both his art and his writings, Russell made it clear that he wished the history had turned out differently.

In one of the Salish-Pend d'Oreille Culture Committee's recorded interviews, tribal elder Pete Beaverhead reviewed Russell's paintings and gave high praise to the artist's work: "All of Russell's pictures are good. He knows the Indian ways good. It is all true. See this—this is Salish or Kalispel. You recognize the clothing. It is their way." (Pete Beaverhead, SPCC OHA 43/1 [1975])

10,000 Years Indigenous People— 200 Years Lewis and Clark, number 7, by Corky Clairmont, 2002.